Contents

NEWTON SPORTS CLUB

Application for membership

Name (Mr/Mrs/Miss) ....
                    (Surname)   (First names)

Address ....

....

....

Telephone No .... Age ....

Occupation ....

Sporting interests: Football ☐   Basketball ☐

                     Hockey   ☐   Gymnastics ☐

                     Swimming ☐   Other ....

                                        ....

Name and Address of) ....
one person willing) ....
to give a character) ....
reference.   )
                       ....

Signed .... Date ....

Commercial Typewriting

Ninth edition

Based on the eighth edition by Aileen M Prince

Pitman

PITMAN PUBLISHING
128 Long Acre, London WC2E 9AN

A Division of Longman Group UK Limited

© Longman Group UK Limited 1988

British Library Cataloguing in Publication Data
Walmsley, William
 Walmsley's Commercial typewriting. — 9th ed.
 1. Typewriting
 I. Title   II. Walmsley, Elizabeth
 652.3   Z49

ISBN 0 273 02898 7

Ninth Edition 1988
Reprinted 1988, 1990, 1992

ISBN Caribbean Edition 0 273 03140 6
First printed 1989
Reprinted 1990, 1992

ISBN East African Edition 0 273 03275 5
First printed 1990

Note. The material on pages 167-170 is copyright free and may
be photocopied for use by the student in carrying out exercises
given in this book.

Produced by Longman Group (FE) Ltd
Printed in Hong Kong

Preface

The ninth edition of *Walmsley's Commercial Typewriting* has been completely revised to bring the work up to date with modern office procedures and the current requirements of examination boards. The text, which follows the structure of the eighth edition, helps you to master the techniques necessary for efficient keyboard operation and the development of a high level of speed and accuracy.

Instructions and exercises in each chapter are carefully graded and clearly presented. As you progress through the book, the detailed guidelines and well-designed range of practical exercises help you to achieve competence in producing well-displayed typewritten material of a mailable standard. A suggested 'Target Time' is provided for each exercise, to develop the production-typing skills necessary in today's office. A range of headed stationery is included to provide realistic practice. These headed papers are copyright-free, and you may photocopy them to use with the exercises in the book.

The material in each chapter progresses from the simple to the complex, introducing and developing typewriting skills to a high level of proficiency. The wide variety of practical tasks in each chapter provide realistic business experience and valuable background information about modern office practice and secretarial procedures.

The requirements of all typewriting examinations, from elementary to advanced stages, are covered in the text, including the recently introduced changes to the Royal Society of Arts examinations.

INVOICE   No.

Avon & Vestry Ltd 701 Nunnery Walk
Birmingham, B4 8NE

Telephone: Birmingham 32687

Sold to: Date:

Your Order No.   Terms: Net 30 days

Quantity	Description	Unit cost	Amount

E & OE

Index

Everton Crouch

Registered Address:
Kenilworth House
Bedford Road
Hemel Hempstead
Herts. HP2 8LJ

Telephone: 0442 17376

- -

MEMORANDUM

From

To   *Date*

Everton Crouch

Registered Address:
Kenilworth House
Bedford Road
Hemel Hempstead
Herts, HP2 8LJ

Telephone: 0442 17376

1 Typewriter parts and their uses

A For keyboard learning

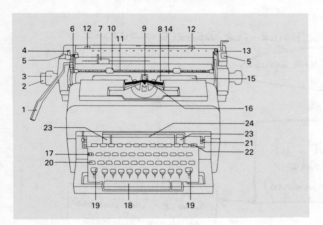 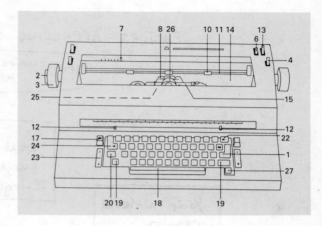

Key

1	Carriage-return lever	10	Paper grips
2	Variable line spacer	11	Paper bail scale
3	Cylinder knobs	12	Margin stops
4	Interliner	13	Paper-release lever
5	Carriage-release levers	14	Platen roller (cylinder)
6	Line-space selector	15	Transparent paper holders
7	Paper guide	16	Printing point indicator
8	Alignment scale	17	Margin-release key
9	Card holder	18	Space bar

19	Shift keys
20	Shift lock
21	Colour change adjuster
22	Back-space key
23	Tabulator set and clear keys
24	Tabulator bar/key
25	Carrier
26	Printing element
27	Half-space correction key (electric & electronic machines)

See the diagrams above for references to the parts.

Back-space key (22) The position of this key varies on different makes of typewriter, and you should find out where it is on your own machine. Its function is to move the printing point one space back.

Carriage-release levers (5) Manual machines only. The levers which, when depressed, allow the carriage to be moved freely to the left and right.

Carriage-return lever or key (1) The lever or key that is used for turning up the paper and for returning the printing point to the left margin in order to begin a new line.

Carrier (25) Many electric/electronic machines have a carrier (incorporating the printing head) which moves across the page, rather than the carriage moving as on a typebar machine.

Cylinder knobs (3) The knobs at each end of the cylinder which move the paper either up or down.

Line-space selector (6) The lever that regulates the depth of the spacing between the lines. It may be set for single-, double- or treble-line spacing (with half-spacing on some machines), and should be adjusted for the required depth before you begin work. (See page 5.)

Margin-release key (17) When depressed, this allows you to type beyond the set margin points at either end of the line.

Margin stops (12) These are used to fix the points at which the lines of typewriting begin on the left and end on the right. As you approach the end of a line a warning bell will ring, after which you may finish a short word or hyphenate a long one and continue on the next line. The keyboard should lock when the carriage has travelled a few spaces after the bell has rung.

Paper bail scale (11) The movable arm, marked with

Exercise 257 (Target time = 25 minutes)

Left margin may be less than 25 mm (1″) but not less than 12 mm (½″). Centre the main heading. This chart was featured in a Stage II Examination of the Royal Society of Arts.

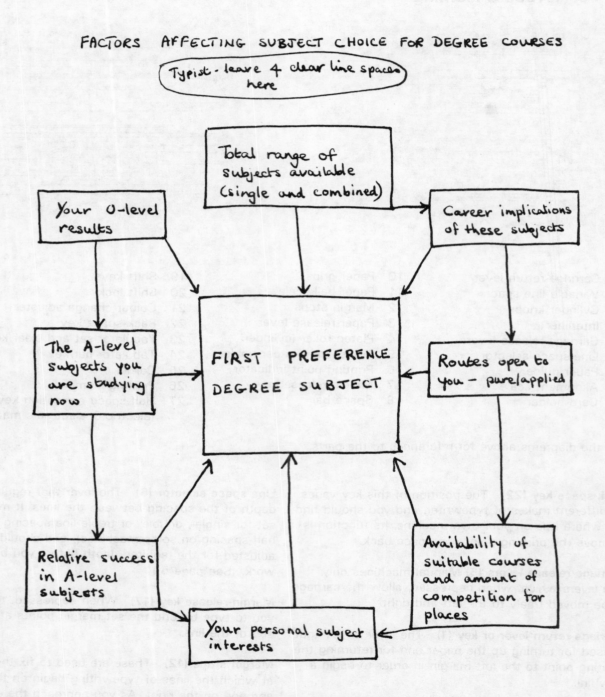

FACTORS AFFECTING SUBJECT CHOICE FOR DEGREE COURSES

Typist - leave 4 clear line spaces here

Total range of subjects available (single and combined)

Your O-level results

Career implications of these subjects

The A-level subjects you are studying now

FIRST PREFERENCE DEGREE SUBJECT

Routes open to you – pure/applied

Relative success in A-level subjects

Availability of suitable courses and amount of competition for places

Your personal subject interests

[Reproduced by permission of Hobsons Limited]

a typing scale, on which the paper grips are mounted.

Paper grips (10) These are the movable rubber rollers on the paper bail which hold the edges of the paper firmly against the platen. They should be set to the required positions before typing begins.

Paper guide (7) The adjustable guide against which the left-hand edge of the paper is positioned as it is inserted in the machine. This guide should normally be set at zero on the scale.

Paper-release lever (13) The lever which, when pulled forward, moves the feed rollers away from the platen. If the paper is fed in obliquely, or too much to the right or left, it can be freely adjusted after pulling forward the paper-release lever. Always use this lever when taking work out of the machine.

Platen (or cylinder) (14) The roller around which the paper is held. When worn or pitted, the platen may be replaced.

Printing elements (electric/electronic) (26) This may be a golf ball head or a daisywheel. These elements move quickly to make the impression on the page. They are usually interchangeable.

Printing point indicator (16) The point where the character is printed.

B For typing displayed work

Card holder (9) The metal section above the centre of the writing line which can be used in conjunction with the transparent paper holders (right- and left-hand) **(15)** to secure cards or thick envelopes.

Colour change adjuster (21) To be set on white when typing stencils.

Interliner (4) The small lever which can be pulled forward to free the platen, without losing the original typing line. Remember that when using the paper release lever, you are not returned to the original typing line.

Scales The various scales on your machine are designed to help you plan your displayed work precisely. They are shown horizontally as paper bail scale **(11)**, and alignment scale **(8)**.

Tabulator set/clear keys (23) These should always be used for tabulated or columnar display. Co-ordinated with the tabulator bar or key **(24)**, they will enable you to display your work accurately and efficiently, without unnecessary tapping of the space bar. When you tap the tab bar, the carriage will stop at whatever tab stops you have set. Be sure to clear your machine of all previous settings before you begin a fresh job.

Golf ball heads

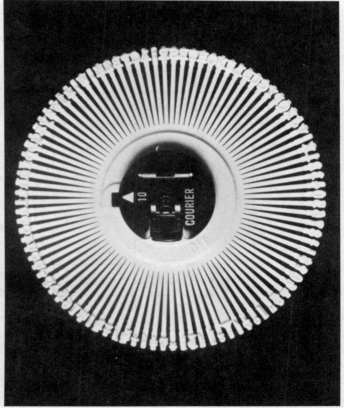

Daisywheel

Typewriter parts and their uses

2

Flow charts

Flow charts indicate the sequence of the various stages in a procedure.

- A variety of symbols may be used. Complicated symbols eg triangles may be drawn in using a template (a special transparent piece of plastic), if the appropriate size of template is available.
- Boxes may be used or simply the wording on its own if the flow chart is simple.
- Boxes may be ruled with equal space around each item, or boxes can be of equal size with items blocked within them.
- Unbroken lines, with arrows, show the flow. These may come from or go to more than one item.
- Type horizontal lines with the underscore, and rule vertical lines with a black pen.
- Broken lines with arrows can be used to indicate feedback/possible repetition of procedure. These should be drawn with a ruler and black pen.
- Layout for flow charts can be varied considerably, provided the chart is clear to the reader, but the order in which the boxes are presented must not be changed.

Exercise 256 (Target time = 15 minutes)

Prepare a typewritten version of the following flow chart. All lines should be drawn with a ruler and pen.

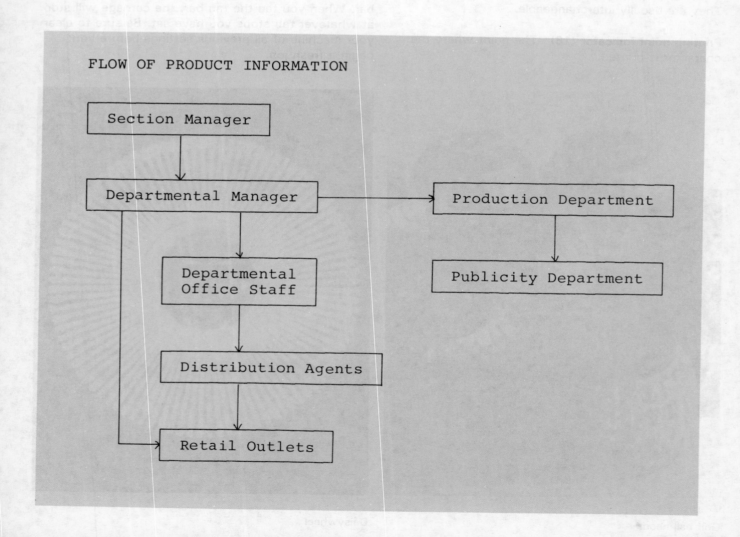

FLOW OF PRODUCT INFORMATION

Touch-control adjuster   A numbered selector for adapting the typewriter to your personal touch-pressure. Check the machine manual for the position of this selector.

Transparent paper holders (15)   These small pieces of plastic, positioned over the writing line, have three uses: *a*   they have an alignment scale, which indicates the bottom of the typing line; *b*   they hold small papers, cards or envelopes in position; and *c*   they enable ruling to be carried out quickly and efficiently. The opening in the paper holder on the left is for the point of a ball-point pen or well-sharpened pencil; the opening at the right is for the point of a stylus used in stencil work. To rule *horizontal* lines, place the point of the pen or pencil in the hole provided and allow the carriage to travel as far as required by using the carriage-release lever; to rule *vertical* lines, pull the interliner forward and then rotate the platen. With practice, this method of ruling can save time.

Variable line spacer (2)   This knob (at the end of the left-hand cylinder knob) can be operated to enable matter to be typed other than on the original writing lines, but you must remember that such an operation changes the original position permanently.

Exercise 255 (Target time = 25 minutes)

Prepare a typewritten version of the following organisation chart on A4 paper.

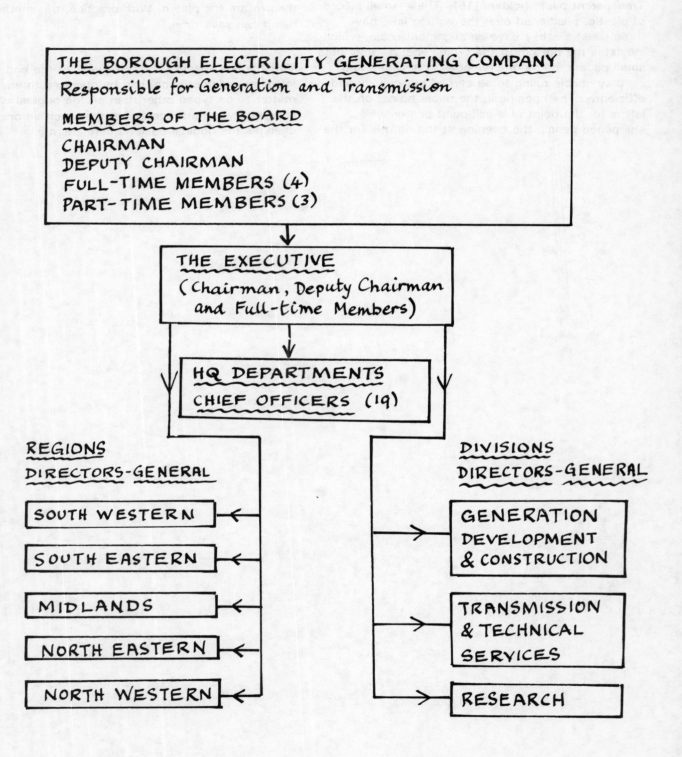

THE BOROUGH ELECTRICITY GENERATING COMPANY
Responsible for Generation and Transmission
MEMBERS OF THE BOARD
CHAIRMAN
DEPUTY CHAIRMAN
FULL-TIME MEMBERS (4)
PART-TIME MEMBERS (3)

THE EXECUTIVE
(Chairman, Deputy Chairman
and Full-time Members)

HQ DEPARTMENTS
CHIEF OFFICERS (19)

REGIONS
DIRECTORS-GENERAL

SOUTH WESTERN
SOUTH EASTERN
MIDLANDS
NORTH EASTERN
NORTH WESTERN

DIVISIONS
DIRECTORS-GENERAL

GENERATION
DEVELOPMENT
& CONSTRUCTION

TRANSMISSION
& TECHNICAL
SERVICES

RESEARCH

2 Keyboard learning

Posture

Efficiency demands a suitable chair and desk, each at the correct height for the operator.

● The typewriter should be level with the front edge of the desk.
● Locate the 'home keys'—ASDF for the left hand and ;LKJ for the right hand. Your fingers always return to these keys.
● Adjust your chair so that when you are seated at the machine with your fingers on the home keys your forearms are sloping slightly upwards.
● Your arms should hang naturally at your sides with the elbows well in.
● Your wrists should be straight (not humped) and your fingers curved.
● Sit well back in your chair, back erect and shoulders down and back. Avoid any stiffness and tension.
● Have both your feet flat on the floor, preferably with one slightly in front of the other to give balance. Never cross your legs or wind them round the chair: the aim is to achieve a comfortable position which will avoid fatigue.

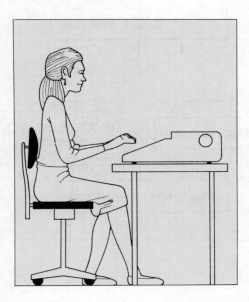

Eyes on copy

Unless you require to hyphenate a word at the end of the line, avoid the temptation to look at your work in the machine. The more you keep your eyes on the copy (or on your notebook), the faster and more accurate you will be.

Correct operation — manual machines

Striking the keys

Curve your fingers and strike each key lightly but firmly and evenly with the finger-tip. Make sure that only one key is struck at a time and allowed to return to the type basket before the next key is struck: this will avoid jamming the keys at the printing point.

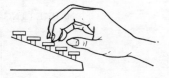

The steep slope of a manual machine requires a tight curve to the fingers

Space bar

Strike the space bar smartly with the right-hand thumb to obtain a space. Make the movement a definite one, the same as for striking a key.

Carriage return

To start a new line, return the carriage using the carriage-return lever: this will simultaneously turn up the paper and return the carriage to the beginning of a new line. Use the left hand (palm downwards), and move the carriage quickly to the right by striking the lever smartly. As soon as the carriage is returned, all the fingers of the left hand must be brought immediately back to their home keys, the right-hand fingers remaining on their home keys during the whole of this operation. Make one sweeping movement from the home keys and back again. Remember to keep your eyes on the copy when returning the carriage.

Organisation charts

An organisation chart shows the relationship between the various areas of an organisation and the comparative levels of responsibility.

- The vertical layout is the most common (as shown in Exercise 254), with the lines of responsibility reading from the top to the bottom. A horizontal chart would read from left to right.
- Positions of equal importance are usually on the same line, but where some lines are too long to fit across the page, the items may be typed on different horizontal lines.
- The items are linked by unbroken lines.
- Boxes are optional, but follow the style shown in the draft or any instructions given.
- Type the horizontal lines with the underscore, and rule the vertical lines with a black pen after the table has been completed. Use pencil marks first then rule final lines. Boxes may be ruled with equal spacing around each item or boxes on the same line may be the same size.
- Calculation of starting points for each item requires the skills learned in Tabulation.
- Centre the chart horizontally and vertically on the page.
- Blocked or centred style may be used.

Exercise 254   (Target time = 15 minutes)

Type the following organisation chart on A4 paper.

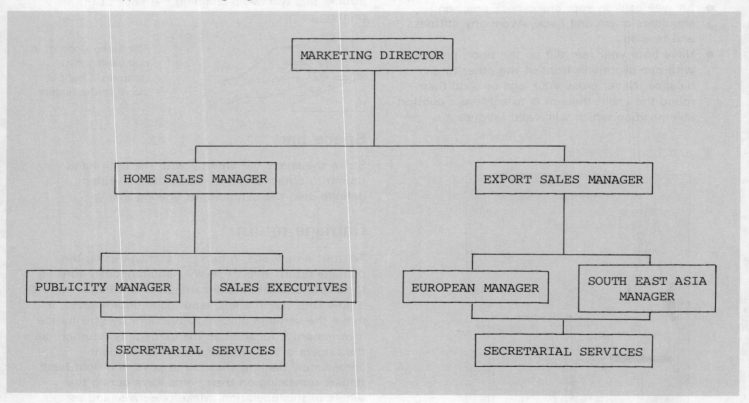

Correct operation — electric and electronic machines

Electric and electronic typewriters (including word processors) are now very widely used in the business office. The most important points to note are as follows.

Striking the keys

The keys do not require striking; they operate at the lightest touch. You therefore do not need to curve your fingers as much as on a manual machine. Your finger-tips should glide from one key to the next and this movement is facilitated by the keyboard being less sloping than on a manual machine. When in the home position your fingers should not actually rest on the home keys, but should hover over them. It is particularly important when operating electric/electronic typewriters that the height of your chair should match the height of the table so that when in their natural position your forearms are at the same slope as the keyboard. Sitting comfortably at all times will be found to minimise fatigue and facilitate high-speed operation.

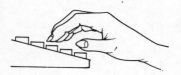

The flatter keyboard on an electric/electronic machine or computer requires less curve to the fingers.

(Carriage) return

There is no carriage-return lever. This dual movement is achieved by operating a *return* or *new line* key which is part of the keyboard and generally located at the right-hand side of the keyboard. This key is operated with the fourth finger of the right hand.

Other differences

Frequently, keys can be repeated, eg a full stop for a dotted line, an x repeated for obliterating unwanted words and a hyphen repeated for a broken line. The space bar and the backspacer will both continue to operate rapidly if kept depressed. There may be a REPEAT key which will repeat all key strokes.

A variety of different typefaces is often available taking only seconds to replace one for another. The mechanism of the machine ensures that all characters are printed with the same degree of impact, so that each character makes an even impression on the paper.

NB In the next section, on Keyboard Learning, look for the 'dagger' (†) in the right-hand margin to remind you of differences in operation.

Line spacing and margins

The line-space selector controls the distance between the lines. It can be adjusted for single-, double- or treble-line spacing, often with half-space settings as well.

Before beginning to type, set the selector for the required spacing. The early exercises should be typed in single-line spacing (no space between lines) so that any mistakes are more readily seen. One space should generally be left between exercises or portions of an exercise — operate the carriage return twice.

The margin stops should be set for the work as indicated at the head of the exercises.

Line 1	This	This	This	This
2	column		(1 space)	(1 space)
3	shows	is	is	(1 space)
4	single	1½	(1 space)	is
5	line		double	(1 space)
6	spacing	spacing	(1 space)	(1 space)
7			spacing	treble

Insertion of the paper

- Use a backing sheet behind ordinary typing paper. It improves the appearance of the work, reduces noise and prevents the paper from being creased.
- To secure a uniform left margin on successive sheets, the paper guide should be set at point zero on the scale.
- Raise the paper bail.
- Take hold of the sheets of paper with the left hand and drop them between the platen and feed rollers with the left-hand edge against the paper guide.
- With the right hand, turn the platen knob until the paper reaches the required position.
- Use the paper-release lever if the paper is not straight.
- Lower the paper bail and adjust the grips to press against the left- and right-hand edges of the paper to hold it firmly against the platen.

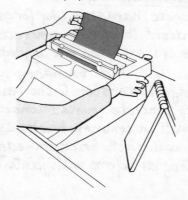

SPECIFICATION of work to be carried out to erect

a proposed garage extension and garden wall at

42 Park Drive, Leston Park, Brighton, E Sussex,

for and to the satisfaction of:

B R Williams, FRIBA
Architect and Surveyor
1210 High Street
Dover Kent   DR6 9BH

21 January 19--

<u>Site Clearance</u>
Cut down and grub up roots of existing trees and remove all from site.

<u>Foundations</u>
Excavate oversite to reduce level to formation of extension.

Excavate foundation trenches and lay concrete (1:3:6) 40 mm aggregate foundations 1' 6" x 9" thick.

Half-brick wall in Warnham common bricks in cement mortar (1:4) where unexposed.

Half-brick wall in Facing bricks to match existing in cement mortar (1:4) with joints rubbed up where unexposed.

4½" wide bituminous felt horizontal dpc

4" thick hardcore bed to receive concrete oversite.

4" thick concrete (1:3:6) 20 mm aggregate oversite.

<u>Walls</u>
Half-brick wall in Facing bricks to match the existing in gauged mortar (1:3:6) with joints rubbed up both sides.

Roof
<u>Construction</u>
All timber to be 'protimized'.
2" x 4" sawn softwood plates.
2" x 4" sawn softwood roof joists at 16" centres.
1" sawn softwood roof boarding with shallow firrings.
<u>Covering</u>
Three layer built-up felt roof
<u>Rainwater Goods</u>
Fix existing and supply new P.V.C. guttering and rainwater pipe where necessary to discharge into a P.V.C. rainwater butt.

EXTERNAL WORKS
<u>Concrete Hardstanding</u>
Lay a concrete hardstanding for garden wheelbarrow, as follows:
4" bed hardcore to receive concrete.
4" concrete (1:3:6:) 20 mm aggregate bed with tamped finish.

BOUNDARY WALL
Construct a 4' 6" high boundary wall to continue from the end of the Garage Extension to the rear boundary as follows:
1' 6" x 9" deep concrete foundations as before.
Half-brick wall in common bricks as before where unexposed.
Half-brick wall with brick-on-edge coping in Facing bricks to match existing as before with joints rubbed up all round.

Removal of the paper

- Raise the paper bail.
- Pull forward the paper-release lever (using the right hand), and remove the paper with the left hand.
- Return the paper bail and the paper-release lever to their normal positions.

Typing by touch

The quickest way to develop your sense of touch is to rely on it. Therefore, do not look at the machine or your work whilst you are typing, except to locate new keys when they are first typed.

Operation of the typewriter is based upon the positioning of fingers on the **home keys**. The keys ASDF are the home keys of the left hand, whilst the keys ;LKJ are the home keys of the right hand. You should be able to find these keys without looking for them. Always return the fingers to these keys after striking another key.

Having learnt the keyboard, as you will in the next few lessons, you will be able to type without taking your eyes from the copy and this saves a great deal of time. It also reduces the risk of inaccuracy which comes from looking away from the copy, namely the omission of words or the repetition of words.

Correct fingering

The keyboard is divided into two parts. Each hand must be used for its own side of the keyboard only. Each finger must be used only for the keys allocated to it. All the fingers are used in operating the typewriter keys, and the right thumb is used for striking the space bar.

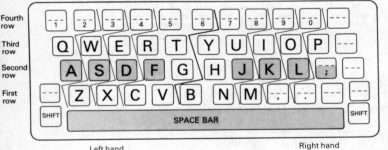

Fourth row
Third row
Second row
First row

Left hand   Right hand

Guide keys and guide fingers: the position of the fingers

The second row of keys contains the guide keys **a** and ; (semicolon). The little finger of the left hand must rest lightly on the **a** and that of the right hand on the ; (semicolon). The little fingers are known as **'guide fingers'** because from their position over their guide keys you are able, by the sense of location, to find the position of any other key.

The other three fingers of the left hand should be placed in order over **s d f**. The remaining fingers of

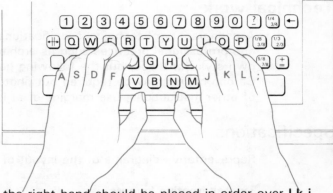

the right hand should be placed in order over **l k j**. The four keys **a s d f** on the left and the four keys **; l k j** on the right, called the **'home' keys**, are for the four fingers of each hand. The respective fingers should remain in these positions when not striking other keys.

Typewriter type

- The typewritten examples in this book are divided between pica type and elite type. Some machines may have 15-pitch.

  10-pitch (pica) gives 10 characters to 1" (25 mm)
  12-pitch (elite) gives 12 characters to 1" (25 mm)
  15-pitch gives 15 characters to 1" (25 mm)

- Pica is used throughout this section.

  This is 10-pitch (pica)
  This is 12-pitch (elite)
  This is 15-pitch

- A typing line of six inches will give sixty letters and spaces in pica along the lines but the same width will accommodate seventy-two letters and spaces in elite.
- There are six lines of typing to the inch vertically for *all* typefaces.

Keyboard exercises

- Remember that your fingers have to do the work. Keep your hands and wrists in the correct position.
- For spaces, strike the bar sharply with the right thumb.
- Where no right-hand margin is given, the right-hand margin stop should be set as far as possible to the right.

Proofreading

Check your work at the end of each exercise. Every wrong key struck is a mistake and the omission of a space or the inclusion of an extra space or character is also a mistake. Circle each mistake in pencil, indicating the number of errors in a circle in the left-hand margin.

Technical work

A wide variety of technical specifications and bills of quantities are used in industry and professional practices such as architects' offices. Many companies have their own style for these, but the following general instructions provide a basic guideline. Carbon copies may be required but photocopying may be preferred. In the absence of other instructions, use margins of at least 25 mm (1").

Specifications

Representative diagrams of the layout of a specification are given below.

Two alternative layouts

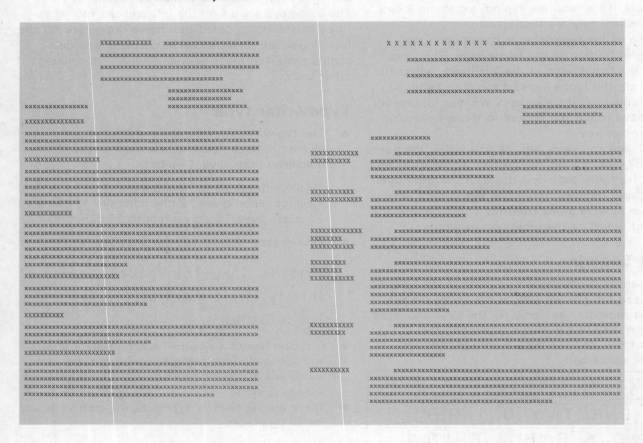

- The first section begins with the word 'specification'. It may be typed in spaced capitals and may protrude to the left, making the first section a 'hanging' paragraph.
- Type the first section in one-and-a-half-line or double-line spacing.
- Below that, on the right, in single-line spacing, is the name and address of the architect, surveyor or customer to whom the specification is addressed.
- The next item is the date.
- Each separate item heading is typed at the left-hand margin, in capitals, generally as side (marginal) headings or as shoulder headings.
- Paragraphs are typed in single-line spacing.

Exercise 253 (Target time = 25 minutes)

Type a copy of the brief specification on the next page, inserting today's date.
Type measurements as shown.

The home keys

The keys for **a s ; l** sometimes present difficulty because the third and fourth fingers are weak. Try to move only the finger that strikes the key. Practice will give freedom of movement, and make these fingers stronger.

Exercise 1

Left margin	`asdf ;lkj asdf ;lkj asdf ;lkj as`
25 pica	`asdf ;lkj asdf ;lkj asdf ;lkj as`
35 elite	`a ad add adds; ask lad all falls`
	`a ad add adds; ask lad all falls`
	`a ad add adds; ask lad all falls`

Are you sitting correctly?

New keys g and h

Exercise 2

The objects of this exercise are to strengthen the use of the third and fourth fingers, and to introduce the letters **g** and **h**.
Remember to move only the **f** finger when striking **g**, and immediately bring it back to **f**. Move only the **j** finger to type **h**. Try not to move any other finger.

Left margin	`fg dg jh kh ag as ;h ;l fg dg jh kh ag as ;h ;l`
20 pica	`fg dg jh kh ag as ;h ;l fg dg jh kh ag as ;h ;l`
25 elite	`fg dg jh kh ag as ;h ;l fg dg jh kh ag as ;h ;l`
	`fg dg jh kh ag as ;h ;l fg dg jh kh ag as ;h ;l`
	`fg dg jh kh ag as ;h ;l fg dg jh kh ag as ;h ;l`
	`fg dg jh kh ag as ;h ;l fg dg jh kh ag as ;h ;l`

Check position of feet, arms and wrists

Individual actors' parts

- It is usual for each actor to have a copy of the full script, which can be marked for the actor's own part.
- When the part is very small it is sometimes necessary for an actor's part to be typed separately.
- Having the part typed in double-line spacing facilitates memorising for some players, especially when long speeches are involved, and in these cases the actor's part may be specially typed. The general rules for typing are the same, but all portions of the script which do not apply to the actor are omitted and replaced by 'cues' (the closing words of the previous speaker). These begin near the middle of the page and are typed as other unspoken lines.
- The size of paper used (A4 or A5) will depend on the size of the part.

Exercise 252   (Target time = 6 minutes)

Type the following part for Portia at the opening of Scene ii Act IV of *The Merchant of Venice*, on A4 paper, and compare it with the same section of the complete script shown in the previous exercise.

T H E   M E R C H A N T   O F   V E N I C E

PORTIA - ACT IV

<u>Scene ii.   Venice.   A Street.   Enter Portia and Nerissa</u>

Enquire the Jew's house out, give him this deed,

And let him sign it: we'll away tonight,

And be a day before our husbands home:

This deed will be well welcome to Lorenzo.

<u>Enter Gratiano</u>

... <u>Your company at dinner</u>.

That cannot be:

His ring I do accept most thankfully;

And so, I pray you, tell him: furthermore,

I pray you, show my youth old Shylock's house.

... <u>to keep for ever</u>.

Thou may'st, I warrant. We shall have old swearing

That they did give the rings away to men;

But we'll outface them, and outswear them too.

Away! make haste: thou know'st where I will tarry.

Exercise 3

This exercise consolidates the work of the preceding two exercises.

'Feel' the
new
reaches
before
typing

```
Left margin  fgf asdf asdfgf jhj ;lkj ;lkjhj fgf jhj asdfgf;
20 pica      fgf asdf asdfgf jhj ;lkj ;lkjhj fgf jhj asdfgf;
25 elite     fgf asdf asdfgf jhj ;lkj ;lkjhj fgf jhj asdfgf;
             a sag hag shag flag flags sash dash lash slash;
             a sag hag shag flag flags sash dash lash slash;
```

Exercise 4

These words contain **g** and **h**. Be sure you return to **f** and **j** respectively, immediately the **g** and **h** have been struck. Move only the fingers necessary to strike the keys.

Note that the 'dagger' (†) sign relates to electric/electronic machines.

Type each
key smartly
†Tap lightly

```
Left margin
10 pica
20 elite
```

```
all add ask ash; sad sag dad fag; had has gas had; jag lad lag;
fall half lass; flag alas dash; hall glad asks; hash gash lash;
glass shall flash; flask halls slash; falls flags galas; shall;
had lads glass flask had lads glass flask had lads glass flask;
halls had gala flags halls had gala flags halls had gala flags;
```

The shift keys

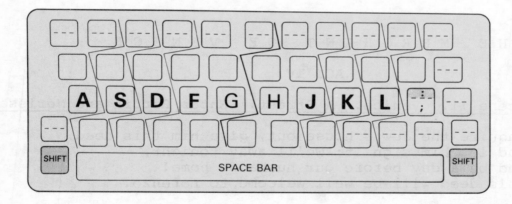

On most machines each key produces two letters or signs: either a small letter and its corresponding capital, or a figure and some other character.

The expression **'lower case'** refers to those characters that may be typed without first operating the shift key, and includes small letters, figures and other common characters. **'Upper case'** refers to those characters typed whilst the shift key is down, and includes the capital letters and other characters not so frequently used.

Using the shift keys

To obtain capital letters and upper-case signs, one of the two shift keys must be operated whilst the character key is struck. When a capital letter on the right-hand side of the keyboard is required, the left-hand shift key must be operated and vice versa.

Typing plays

Plays for theatre, radio or television are typed on A4 paper, on one side of the sheet only. Always take a carbon copy in the absence of any other instructions.

- The front sheet of a typescript contains the titles of the play and the author's name, followed by any sub-title or other short descriptions containing a reference to the period and location of the setting of the story.
  A synopsis is often included, followed by a 'cast list' (list of characters) and, for television, a list of 'sets' (scenes) and film sequences, and the estimated running time.
- In the main body of the script, the names of the characters should be shown in full throughout the play, always in capitals as side headings. All unspoken matter should also be distinguished from the actual dialogue by:
  a underscoring, b enclosing in brackets, or c typing in red if you have a 2-colour (bi-chrome) ribbon.
- In the scripts of plays for radio, it is usual to number each separate item of dialogue consecutively at the left margin. An extra clear line space should be left between parts and sections of dialogue and to separate these from any unspoken matter, including the author's descriptions of sound effects required and other technical directions. For television, scripts contain detailed technical instructions and are typed in two columns with the dialogue on the right.
- The left margin must be wide enough to ensure that all pages remain easily readable although securely fixed together — at least 38 mm (1½"). Number pages consecutively from beginning to end.

When completed, the script may be bound in durable covers.

Exercise 251 (Target time = 10 minutes)

Type a copy of the following opening of a scene in a theatre play on A4 paper.

T H E   M E R C H A N T   O F   V E N I C E

ACT IV

<u>Scene ii.   Venice.   A Street.   Enter Portia and Nerissa</u>

PORTIA   Enquire the Jew's house out, give him this deed,
And let him sign it; we'll away tonight,
And be a day before our husbands home:
This deed will be well welcome to Lorenzo.

<u>Enter Gratiano</u>

GRATIANO   Fair sir, you are well overta'en:
My lord Bassanio, upon more advice,
Hath sent you here this ring; and doth entreat
Your company at dinner.

PORTIA   That cannot be:
His ring I do accept most thankfully;
And so, I pray you, tell him: furthermore,
I pray you, show my youth old Shylock's house.

GRATIANO   That will I do.

NERISSA   Sir, I would speak with you.   (<u>Aside to Portia</u>)   I'll
see if I can get my husband's ring,

A common error on the part of learners is either to depress the shift key insufficiently, or to release the finger from the key just as the type is printing. This causes the upper-case character to be out of line with the others, and sometimes a partial impression of both upper- and lower-case type appears. The correct operation of the shift key should be well practised, not only to prevent the faults mentioned above, but to develop speed.

To type J
1 Hold down the left shift key with the little finger of the left hand
2 Strike the letter **J**
3 Release the shift key
4 Return all fingers of the left hand to the home keys

● The shift key must be fully depressed and held firmly until the capital letter has been struck.
● Once the letter has been typed, the fingers must return immediately to the home keys.

Exercise 5

Left margin
25 pica
35 elite

```
Aa Ss Dd Ff Gg Hh Jj Kk Ll :;
Aa Ss Dd Ff Gg Hh Jj Kk Ll :;
aA sS dD fF gG hH jJ kK lL ;:
aA sS dD fF gG hH jJ kK lL ;:
A; Ls Dk Jf Gh :a Sl Kd Fj Hg
Da Fl Sa Gs Jk Lf Kd Sh Al Ha
```

New keys e and i

● Move the finger from **d** to **e**, strike it sharply, and return to **d**. The finger on **k** is moved similarly to strike **i**.
● The fingers should rest on the home keys, and it is necessary to keep the little fingers upon the guide keys as **e** and **i** are struck.
● One finger only should be moved away from the home keys at a time. Return it when the letter has been struck.

Exercise 6

Left margin
25 pica
35 elite

```
ded kik ded kik ded kik ded kik;
ded kik ded kik ded kik ded kik;
fed hid led ail sea his leg aid;
lea fig see lid fee jig keg die;
dee did lee dig eel lie egg gig;
```

Fingers
curved
†Fingers
slightly
curved

Literary work

Margins Literary work is usually typed with a left-hand margin of at least 38 mm (1½″) so that all sheets can be fastened together but easily read, and a right-hand margin of 25 mm (1″) is normal.

Spacing Double-line spacing is used if revision is expected, as this leaves sufficient space between the lines for alterations or additions; but one-and-a-half-line spacing is generally acceptable for a final typing. Synopses, extracts and footnotes, however, are usually typed in single-line spacing to make them stand out clearly.

Pagination The first page of a novel, story or article is not numbered, as the heading shows that it is the first page; and the introduction or preface may be numbered in small roman numerals. The remaining pages should be numbered consecutively in arabic numerals and these may be at the left or right margin, or centred, about 13 mm (½″) from the top.

The work must be well arranged, with plenty of space at the top and bottom of each page. Some sections may be in 'hanging paragraph' form — with the second and subsequent lines indented two or three spaces. All spelling, capitalisation, use of words and figures, numbering or lettering of sections, and the number of lines of type on full pages should be consistent.

Typing poetry

Follow these guidelines, unless given specific instructions.

- Poetry should be typed in single-line spacing, centred horizontally and vertically on the page, unless it is part of a longer document.
- Most poems have a capital letter at the beginning of each line.
- When alternate lines rhyme, they are sometimes indented two or three spaces to the right — the indentation must be consistent.
- No indentations are made when successive lines rhyme, or when the lines do not rhyme at all.
- It is essential that you follow the exact punctuation and capitalisation as given in the copy.

Exercise 250   (Target time = 5 minutes)

Type the following verses from 'Winter' by Robert Burns. Follow the spelling shown. Centre horizontally and vertically on A5 paper.

```
The wintry west extends his blast,
   And hail and rain does blaw;
Or the stormy north sends driving forth
   The blinding sleet and snaw:
Wild-tumbling brown, the burn comes down,
   And roars frae bank to brae:
While bird and beast in covert rest,
   And pass the heartless day.

'The sweeping blast, the sky o'ercast,'
   The joyless winter day
Let others fear, to me more dear
   Than all the pride of May:
The tempest's howl, it soothes my soul,
   My griefs it seems to join;
The leafless trees my fancy please,
   Their fate resembles mine!
```

Exercise 7

This exercise improves the action of the third and fourth fingers.
Concentrate your attention on two things: moving each finger independently of any other, and returning it to its home key promptly.

Left margin	de se ki li ae af ;i ;j de se ki li ae af ;i ;j	Keep your
20 pica	de se ki li ae af ;i ;j de se ki li ae af ;i ;j	eyes
25 elite	de se ki li ae af ;i ;j de se ki li ae af ;i ;j	always on
	de se ki li ae af ;i ;j de se ki li ae af ;i ;j	the copy
	de se ki li ae af ;i ;j de se ki li ae af ;i ;j	
	de se ki li ae af ;i ;j de se ki li ae af ;i ;j	

Exercise 8

Remember to return your fingers to the home keys.
Do not forget to strike the space bar smartly at the end of each word.

Left margin	aside files ideal liked slide skill isles agile	Let your
20 pica	aside files ideal liked slide skill isles agile	fingers
25 elite	aside files ideal liked slide skill isles agile	'bounce'
	deeds jaded lease edged legal hedge false shell	off the
	deeds jaded lease edged legal hedge false shell	keys
	Edale Iliad Elias Delia Lille Adela Hilda Slade	†Tap lightly

Exercise 9

The following sentences will give you practice on the shift keys and the letters **e** and **i**. No full stops are shown because you have not yet learnt this key reach.

Left margin	A glass shelf is ideal	Relax—
25 pica	she likes a seaside sail	avoid all
35 elite	His saddle is safe if held	tension
	He said I held a legal lease	
	Eddie said I fell as I skidded	

New keys r t u and y

Take your time when new letters are introduced to get used to the position of the keys. The movement to and from each key should be quick and a part of the act of striking. Return your fingers to the home keys immediately after striking the new keys.

Leaflets

Paper may be used unfolded, or folded to form different size sheets.

Using folded sheets

- The pages may be used portrait or landscape. The decision will depend upon the matter to be typed and the writer's instructions.
- Before beginning to type, lightly mark the pages with pencil so that you will not forget which is the front (F or 1) back (B or 4) inside left (IL or 2) and inside right (IR or 3). Remember to erase these pencil marks from your finished work.
- Always place a sheet of thick paper between the sheets when typing on a folded sheet or type with sheet opened out if possible.
- The 2 inside pages will be viewed together, so display should be well-balanced.

Exercise 249 (Target time = 20 minutes)

Type the following.

The following information is to be typed as a 4 page programme.
Use a single sheet of A4 paper folded in half to form a leaflet.

FRONT PAGE CAPS.

The Phoenix Players
Present
The Merchant of Venice
by
William Shakespeare

Left-hand inside page

The Action of the play takes place
partly at Venice & partly at Belmont,
the seat of Portia, on the Continent.

ACT I   Venice. A Street.
ACT II   Belmont. A Room in Portia's House.
ACT III Venice. A Street.
ACT IV   Venice. A Court of Justice.
ACT V   Belmont. The Avenue to Portia's House.

Right-hand inside page

Characters

Antonio, the Merchant of Venice .. .. .. John Osborn
Bassanio, his friend .. .. Henry Williams
Shylock, a Jew - - - - Geoffrey Watts
Portia, a rich Heiress - — — Mary Briggs
Nerissa, her waiting maid - — — Jean Tippl
Jessica, daughter of Shylock - — — Susan Hunt

foot of back page   Printed by
L. Wilson & Sons Ltd.
London. W1

Exercise 10

Left margin									
25 pica	frf	ftf	juj	jyj	frf	ftf	juj	jyj;	
35 elite	frf	ftf	juj	jyj	frf	ftf	juj	jyj;	
	red	get	yes	hug	rid	yet	dye	due;	
	her	ate	say	hue	sir	fit	fly	hut;	
	are	the	hay	fur	rat	its	day	rue;	

Wrists
straight
not
humped

Exercise 11

The object of this exercise is to help you to find the new letters.

Left margin
20 pica
25 elite

```
dr fr ku ju fg ft jh jy dr fr ku ju fg ft jh jy
dr fr ku ju fg ft jh jy dr fr ku ju fg ft jh jy
dr fr ku ju fg ft jh jy dr fr ku ju fg ft jh jy
dr fr ku ju fg ft jh jy dr fr ku ju fg ft jh jy
dr fr ku ju fg ft jh jy dr fr ku ju fg ft jh jy
dr fr ku ju fg ft jh jy dr fr ku ju fg ft jh jy
```

Sit erect
and well
back

Exercise 12

Typing these words will give you more practice on all the keys learnt so far.
Pay particular attention to the use of the shift key in the last line.

Left margin
25 pica
35 elite

```
rifle these utter yield reads three
udder yeast light great seedy hurly
daily freed gates third greet flies
yards gaily there heart jaded feeds
Reuss Terry Uriah Yates Titus Reide
```

Are you
mastering
every
exercise?

Exercise 13

Keep your eyes and mind entirely on the words you are copying. Do not leave any
line until you have completed a correct typing.

Left margin
20 pica
25 elite

```
Ruth has a stylish fur hat
The largest freight is there
Letters are filed here regularly
Usually she garages it at this address
They had a great yield at this estate earlier
```

Return the
carriage
smartly
†Tap key
with little
finger

New keys q w p and o

Exercise 247 (Target time = 15 minutes)

Type each of the examples below on a separate sheet of paper.

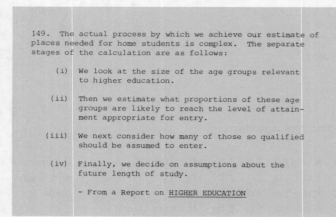

149. The actual process by which we achieve our estimate of places needed for home students is complex. The separate stages of the calculation are as follows:

(i) We look at the size of the age groups relevant to higher education.

(ii) Then we estimate what proportions of these age groups are likely to reach the level of attainment appropriate for entry.

(iii) We next consider how many of those so qualified should be assumed to enter.

(iv) Finally, we decide on assumptions about the future length of study.

- From a Report on HIGHER EDUCATION

CONTENTS

Accents

For typing in foreign languages, certain accent signs are necessary. When a machine is to be used largely for foreign correspondence it may be fitted with the required accents. These are:

´ (acute)　　　　` (grave)　　　　ˆ (circumflex)　　　　¨ (diaeresis or umlaut)

In addition to these the following complete characters are required:

ç (cedilla)　　ñ (tilde)

As manual typewriters are built to a standard size, it is not possible to extend the type basket and the keyboard to make room for these extra characters. The only means of accommodating them is by dispensing with some other characters that are less likely to be wanted, such as the fractions. Daisywheels, used on electronic typewriters, can be changed to extend the range of characters.

The normal practice is to fit the accents to 'dead' keys, which do not act on the carriage-spacing escapement, so that the accent is printed on striking the key but the carriage does not move to the left. On this kind of machine the 'dead' (accent) key is struck first and then the letter.

If the accents are not fitted to 'dead' keys, the letter over which the accent is to be placed should be typed first, and then the backspacer used to return the carriage one space. The required accent is then typed over the character.

When a machine is not provided with accent signs they may be inserted afterwards in matching ink, but the result is not as satisfactory in appearance as when the signs are typed.

Exercise 248 (Target time = 15 minutes)

Type the following Glossary of terms. Leave a clear line space between items. Type items in alphabetical order.

GLOSSARY
Crême de Banane — a banana-flavoured liqueur
Crême de Cacao — a chocolate and vanilla-flavoured liqueur
Pétillant — slightly sparkling
Añada — a Spanish term meaning a vintage wine
Pousse Café — a liqueur of anisette, Curaçao and cacao
Crême de Noyaux — an almond-flavoured liqueur
Premières Côtes de Bordeaux — a wine-growing region of France
Edelgewächs — a German term meaning "a noble wine"
Curaçao — a liqueur made from the peel of dried green oranges
Appellation Contrôlée — wines entitled to geographical names
Designacão do origem — comparable with the French Apellation Contrôlée
Cariñena — an area in Spain noted for its rosados wine
Crême de Menthe — a mint-flavoured liqueur
Erzeuger Abfüllung — a German term meaning "bottled by the producers"

You are now ready to use the keys **q w p** and **o**. Do not allow your wrists to twist round in order to reach the new keys. Move only the finger that is needed to strike the key. See that your little fingers hover over the guide keys, except when striking the other keys that are allotted to them. Keep your finger movements quick.

Exercise 14

Left margin
25 pica
35 elite

```
aqa  sws  ;p;  lol  aqa  sws  ;p;  lol;
quo  was  per  oil  qua  seq  top  ode;
que  tow  ply  too  qui  wit  pip  our;
tap  sow  rip  pot  lip  owe  pie  pod;
awe  oat  sap  woe  apt  pit  asp  toe;
```

Use a
staccato
touch
†Use a
light tap

Exercise 15

This exercise concentrates upon the development of the third and fourth fingers. Try to use each finger independently of the others and to keep the little finger of each hand hovering over the guide key as a focal point from which all other keys are located.

Left margin
20 pica
25 elite

```
aw qa ;o p;  aw qa ;o p;  aw qa ;o p;  aw qa ;o p;
aw qa ;o p;  aw qa ;o p;  aw qa ;o p;  aw qa ;o p;
aw qa ;o p;  aw qa ;o p;  aw qa ;o p;  aw qa ;o p;
aw qa ;o p;  aw qa ;o p;  aw qa ;o p;  aw qa ;o p;
aw qa ;o p;  aw qa ;o p;  aw qa ;o p;  aw qa ;o p;
aw qa ;o p;  aw qa ;o p;  aw qa ;o p;  aw qa ;o p;
```

Are your
elbows in?

Exercise 16

You must associate **q w e r** and **t** with the guide key **a** upon which your little finger should rest. Notice that the little finger leaves **a** only to strike **q** and then returns to act as a guide to the further movements of the hand. Similarly, you must associate **p o i u** and **y** with the guide key **;** (semicolon). After every stroke all the fingers should return to the home keys.

Left margin
20 pica
25 elite

```
quality weather through yielded orderly forward
propose usually opposed phrases queried thought
yellows partial whether shipper torture offered
prepare repeats thrills pursues outfits purpose
Quarles Walpole Paisley Ophelia Wardlow Phyliss
```

Strike the
space bar
sharply
† Strike
lightly

Quotation marks

When typing all literary work, pay special attention to single and double quotation marks.

- Use single or double quotation marks for ordinary quotations and the alternative when one quotation appears within another.
- The quotation marks are usually placed outside the comma, question mark, full stop, etc, eg, ''Yes,'' said William, ''I will be at the show.''
- If a sentence is not a complete quotation, but merely ends with a title in quotation marks the full stop is placed outside the quotation marks, eg, I bought ''The Times''.
- When typing several paragraphs of quoted prose, quotation marks are used at the *beginning* of each paragraph and at the *end* of the last, but when quoting poetry the marks appear only at the beginning of the *first* verse and at the end of the *last* one.

Roman numerals

Roman numerals may be typed in upper or lower case (depending on what they are being used for). When a numeral is followed by one of equal or less value, it is added as: VI = 6; XV = 15; LI = 51; CV = 105. When a numeral is preceded by one of less value, it is subtracted as: IV = 4; XL = 40. A line drawn over a large roman numeral multiplies it by one thousand.

Exercise 246 (Target time = 15 minutes)

Type the examples below, in three columns as shown.

Arabic (Ranged left)	Capital Roman (Ranged left)	Small Roman (Ranged right)	Arabic (Ranged left)	Capital Roman (Ranged left)	Small Roman (Ranged right)
1	= I	= i	30	= XXX	= xxx
2	= II	= ii	40	= XL	= xl
3	= III	= iii	50	= L	= l
4	= IV	= iv	60	= LX	= lx
5	= V	= v	70	= LXX	= lxx
6	= VI	= vi	80	= LXXX	= lxxx
7	= VII	= vii	90	= XC	= xc
8	= VIII	= viii	100	= C	= c
9	= IX	= ix	101	= CI	= ci
10	= X	= x	120	= CXX	= cxx
11	= XI	= xi	200	= CC	= cc
12	= XII	= xii	300	= CCC	= ccc
13	= XIII	= xiii	400	= CD	= cd
14	= XIV	= xiv	500	= D	= d
15	= XV	= xv	600	= DC	= dc
16	= XVI	= xvi	700	= DCC	= dcc
17	= XVII	= xvii	800	= DCCC	= dccc
18	= XVIII	= xviii	900	= CM	= cm
19	= XIX	= xix	1,000	= M	= m
20	= XX	= xx	6,000	= $\overline{\text{VI}}$	= $\overline{\text{vi}}$
21	= XXI	= xxi	1,000,000	= $\overline{\text{M}}$	= $\overline{\text{m}}$

- **Large roman numerals** (capital letters) are used in numbers after the names of monarchs; as class or form numbers; in showing the number of a year, a chapter in a book or an act in a play; and in enumerating paragraphs when it is inconvenient to use arabic figures:

  Edward V   Henry VIII   Form III   CHAPTER XIV   ACT IV   MCMLXXVI (1976)
- **Small roman numerals** are used for numbering preliminary pages in books and typescripts, sub-paragraphs, etc.
- Both large and small numerals may be ranged to the left or right consistently in a document.

Exercise 17

You should begin to feel your fingers moving towards the keys without conscious thought and mistakes should be rare. This feeling is the beginning of touch typing. If you still need to improve your finger movement, exercise your third and fourth fingers independently, tapping on the desk with them while the rest of your fingers remain stationary.

Left margin
20 pica
25 elite

```
Quote separately for the upright types please
Without railways people prefer to use airways
Paul requested the typist to order the papers
Other postage rates operate for earlier dates
He requires you to sit quietly whilst we wait
```

New keys c v n and b

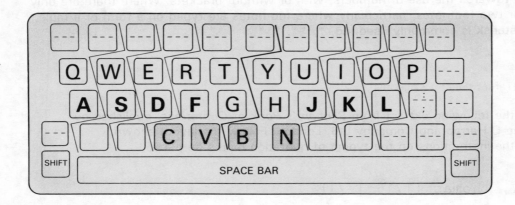

Remember to move only the finger concerned with the key to be struck, and not to move the wrist, which should be kept in its correct position.

Exercise 18

Left margin
25 pica
35 elite

```
fcf fvf jnj jbj fcf fvf jnj jbj;
cab cob ace cub can act car cry;
van vat ave vie vow eve vet ivy;
net nap new nib non now nil nut;
ban bin bar job but rob bus bob;
```

Are your
feet firmly
on the
floor?

Exercise 19

This simple exercise links up the striking of the new keys with the home keys.

Left margin
20 pica
25 elite

```
dc fc kn jn fg fv jh jb dc fc kn jn fg fv jh jb
dc fc kn jn fg fv jh jb dc fc kn jn fg fv jh jb
dc fc kn jn fg fv jh jb dc fc kn jn fg fv jh jb
dc fc kn jn fg fv jh jb dc fc kn jn fg fv jh jb
dc fc kn jn fg fv jh jb dc fc kn jn fg fv jh jb
dc fc kn jn fg fv jh jb dc fc kn jn fg fv jh jb
```

Return to
home keys
promptly

- The footnote sign or number should be typed close up to the word it refers to in the text. Leave at least 1 character space between the footnote sign or number and the start of the footnote itself.
- If the footnote extends to 2 or more lines, type as a blocked paragraph.

2 As an alternative layout, all footnotes may be 'collected together' and typed at the end of a report or a chapter of a book.

3 Work which is being prepared for the printer may incorporate the footnotes within the text, immediately following the text containing the reference to which they are related. It is then the printer's job to place them at the foot of the appropriate page when the page of print is set up.

- Type a line of underscore above and below the footnote, leaving one clear line space above and below each line.
- Use single-line spacing for the footnotes, whatever line spacing is used for the main body of the text.

A variety of reference symbols may be used, eg, *, §, ‡, ‡ Alternatively, lower case letters (a, b, c, d) may be used, with or without brackets. Modern practice tends towards the use of numbers, with or without brackets. Where there are only one or two footnotes, particularly where footnotes are typed on a form or a table, the asterisk is commonly used, eg, *, **, ***.

Exercise 245 (Target time = 12 minutes)

Type the following extract from *Benham's Book of Quotations,* published by George C Harrap and Company Ltd, London. Follow the layout shown.
Read the instructions on the typing of quotation marks on p.155.

```
GRAY, Thomas (1716-1771)

The curfew tolls the knell of parting day,
   The lowing herd winds slowly o'er the lea,*
              - Elegy in a Country Churchyard (1751).
                 solemn
And all the air a/stillness holds.‡              Ib

The moping owl does to the Moon complain.‡      Ib

Await alike th' inevitable hour,§
   The paths of glory lead but to the grave.     Ib
_____

* "The lowing herds wind." - 1st Ed

‡ "There reigned a solemn stillness over all."

                     - Spenser: Faerie Queene

‡ "The wailing owl
   Screams solitary to the mornful moon."

                     - Mallet: Excursion (c 1740)

§ "Ah me! what boots us all our boasted power,
    Our golden treasure, and our purple state.
  They cannot ward the inevitable hour, ..."

       - Richd West: Monody on Queen Caroline (1737)
```

Exercise 20

Typing these words will consolidate your work on the keyboard so far.

Left margin
20 pica
30 elite

```
correct changes conveys request cruelty develop
diverse valuing nothing jocular transit inquiry
opulent sharpen benefit because backing beckons
notable binding cancels dangers naughty between
Chester Valerie Norwich Banbury Charlie Vandyke
```

Type each
key smartly
† Tap lightly

Exercise 21

Type these sentences with care and then repeat them at your highest speed.

Left margin
20 pica
30 elite

```
These vintage vehicles will be abandoned
See your banker about your current account
Brown varnish is often sold over the counter
Never leave any typewriting drills uncorrected
The object will be whitened to avoid an accident
```

Return the
carriage
smartly

New keys z x m comma and full stop

The semicolon, full stop and comma may require a lighter touch if you are using a manual machine. You should inspect the back of the paper and modify your touch if the paper is badly indented.

Note that **z** is typed with the third finger, **x** with the second finger of the left hand.

Exercise 22

Left margin
20 pica
30 elite

```
szsws dxded kmkik l,lol ;.;p; sz dx km l, ;.
szsws dxded kmkik l,lol ;.;p; sz dx km l, ;.
zero, axle, make, lazy, oxen, maps, haze, km
sizes extra mixed zebra extol lamps dizzy sz
zonal boxes milks spitz xylem looms xebec dx
```

Concen-
trate on
correct
key-striking

Footnotes

The layout for footnotes varies, depending on the purpose to which the typescript will be put.

Exercise 244 (Target time = 12 minutes)

Type the following passage. Follow the spelling used in the text. Use double-line spacing for the first paragraph. Follow the layout shown for the lines of poetry. Read the notes below before beginning to type.

<u>EXTRACT FROM BOSWELL'S LIFE OF JOHNSON</u>

It appears from his notes of the state of his mind[1] that he suffered great perturbation and distraction in 1768. Nothing of his writings was given to the publick this year, except the Prologue to his friend Goldsmith's comedy of 'The Good-natured Man' The first lines of this Prologue are strongly character-istical of the dismal gloom of his mind; which in his case, as in the case of all who are distressed with the same malady of imagination, transfers to others its own feelings. Who could suppose it was to introduce a comedy, when Mr Bensley solemnly began,

> 'Press'd with the load of life, the wearing mind
> Surveys the general toil of human kind.'

But this dark ground might make Goldsmith's humour shine the more.[2]

_____

(1)   Prayers and Meditations, p 81.

(2)   In this prologue, as Mr John Taylor informs me, after the fourth line - 'And social sorrow loses half its pain', the following couplet was inserted:

> '<u>Amidst the toils of this returning year</u>
> <u>When senators and nobles learn to fear</u>;
> Our little bard without complain may share
> The bustling season's epidemick care.'

1   In general work the footnotes are typed on the same page as the reference in the text to which they are related. The footnotes are separated from the main body of the text by an underscored line.

- Ensure that you leave enough space at the foot of the page in which to type the footnote(s).
- Type the underscored separating line from edge to edge, or from margin to margin, of the paper.
- Leave at least one clear line space before the separating line, and at least one clear line space between the separating line and the footnote(s).
- Type footnotes in single-line spacing, whatever line spacing is used for the main body of the work.
- Leave one clear line space between footnotes.
- The footnote sign or number should be raised above the normal line of type by half a space in the text. The sign or number does not need to be raised in the footnote itself.

Exercise 23

Note that, in normal punctuation, one space is left after a comma or semicolon, and two after a full stop at the end of a sentence.

Left margin 10 pica, 20 elite

```
zealous realize breezes puzzled assizes gazette zigzags oxidize
maximum explain texture extreme exceeds expects expense example
minimum company members margins morning summary compare mention
zenith, seized, exempt, extent, prefix, suffix, manual, manage,
azure. zebra. among. money. remit. extra. excel. months.
Zachary Xanthus Maureen Zwingli Zambian Xiphias Morpeth Zenobia
```

Exercise 24

This exercise gives you an opportunity of perfecting your finger movements where necessary. The wrists must not be twisted round to reach the bottom row. The little fingers should now be poised above the guide keys all the time, the fingers curved correctly over the keys and an easy rhythmic carriage-return movement maintained.

Left margin
20 pica
25 elite

```
He is certain the size of box will be too small.
She was so lax that more than a dozen were lost.
We have told him to value the zinc in six boxes.
The committee has found this tax cannot be met.
The men in the zone may fix the machine in time.
They can organize the work and then mix the wax.
```

Sit erect and well back

Exercise 25

Do not be satisfied until your fingers move independently and with precision.

Left margin
20 pica
25 elite

```
The result of his call will be known next week.
There may still be time to finish all the work.
I think it may have a very bad effect on sales.
Many in that crowd were unable to see the game.
Quick touch lends speed to my hands at my work.
Quiet study helps them; noise would worry most.
```

Are your eyes on the copy all the time?

Exercise 26

This exercise provides revisionary work on the shift keys and should now present no difficulty.

The metric system

Length

The **metre (m)** is the basic unit and is slightly more than 3 ft 3 in. Type '5 m' for five metres.

The **centimetre (cm)** is one-hundredth of a metre. Type 5 cm for five centimetres, but the same measurement could also be shown as 0.05 m.

The **millimetre (mm)** is one-thousandth of a metre and is very commonly used in some trades. Type 20 mm for 20 millimetres.

The **kilometre (km)** is one thousand metres; about five-eighths of a mile. Type 3 km for three kilometres.

Weight

The **kilogram (kg)** is the basic unit and is slightly less than 2¼ lb. Type 21 kg for 21 kilograms. A **gram (g)** is one-thousandth of a kilogram and a **tonne (t)** is one thousand kilograms. The correct symbol is 't' but as this can be mistaken for an Imperial ton, it is safer to use 'tonne' or even 'metric tonne' (plural, tonnes).

Liquid

The **litre** is the basic unit and is slightly more than 1¾ pints. Five litres is correctly shown as 5 l, but in typewriting 'l' (letter el) could be misread as figure 1 and it is therefore generally safer to type '5 litres'. A **decilitre (dl)** is one-tenth of a litre; a **centilitre (cl)** is one-hundredth of a litre; and a **millilitre (ml)** is one-thousandth of a litre.

Temperature

The everyday metric unit of measurement is the **degree Celsius (°C)**, formerly Centigrade. The boiling point of water is 100 °C and freezing point is 0 °C. The normal human body temperature of 98.4 °F is now correctly typed as 37 °C.

Spacing

Type the number then a space before the symbol, eg, 5 m.

Prefixes

One of the essential features of the system is the use of prefixes to the names of main units and it is important that you should know what they mean and the symbols used for them. These prefix symbols should always be typed close up to the main unit symbol; if you leave a space you will cause confusion, for example, 'mg' means 'milligram' but 'm g' would mean 'metre gram' and would make no sense.

Exercise 242   (Target time = 10 minutes)

Type the above material.

Exercise 243   (Target time = 8 minutes)

Type a copy of the following table. Write the symbol μ in ink.

METRIC PREFIXES

Prefix	Meaning	Symbol	Prefix	Meaning	Symbol
mega	1 million times	M	deci	one-tenth	d
kilo	1 thousand times	k	centi	one-hundredth	c
hecto	1 hundred times	h	milli	one-thousandth	m
deca	ten times	da	micro	one-millionth	μ

Keep your eyes closely on the copy and aim for perfection at the first time of typing.

Left margin																	Hold shift
20 pica	Aq	Sw	De	Fr	Gt	Hy	Ju	Ki	Lo	:p	Aq	Sw	De	Fr	Gt	Hy	keys down
25 elite	Qa	Ws	Ed	Rf	Tg	Yh	Uj	Ik	Ol	P;	Qa	Ws	Ed	Rf	Tg	Yh	firmly
	Aa	Sz	Dx	Fc	Gv	Hb	Jn	Km	L,	Aa	Sz	Dx	Fc	Gv	Hb	Jn	
	aA	Zs	Xd	Cf	Vg	Bh	Nj	Mk	,L	aA	Zs	Xd	Cf	Vg	Bh	Nj	
	So	As	To	Be	In	We	Go	On	Pa	An	Up	No	Me	He	Do	It	

Exercise 27

This exercise will give you additional shift-key practice on every letter of the alphabet.

Left margin
15 pica
25 elite

```
Thomas Hobart lives in Quebec but wants to move to Africa.
David, Eileen and Robert plan to go to Ulster next Friday.
Birmingham and Liverpool are very large industrial cities.
After seeing Russia I hope to go on to Germany and Zambia.
Xanthippe was the wife of Socrates, the Greek philosopher.
On the first Monday in August I shall see Walter in India.
Norma Carter goes to France each year to visit her sister.
Victor Jones will go to Oxford University instead of York.
```

Alphabetic sentences (blocked paragraphs)

Each of the following sentences contains all the letters of the alphabet and should be copied several times, line for line, after setting a left margin at 10 pica, 20 elite. As presented, they each form paragraphs and are in the style known as **blocked** which means that each line begins at the left-hand margin. Always leave extra space between the paragraphs. In single spacing leave one clear space. In double spacing leave three clear spaces.

Exercise 28

```
If you have ambition and are enthusiastic, you will quickly
succeed in joining the company of the experts who have
become wizards of the keys.

Do not be discouraged just because you find a particular
exercise to be extra difficult; you may have tried to type
too quickly without realizing that accuracy comes first.
```

Exercise 29

```
Dexterity in the vocation of typewriting may be acquired by
judicious work and zealous effort.

In consequence of his love of luxury, the wealthy journalist
did not take part in the mountain climb that the young
people organized.
```

Exercise 239 (Target time = 10 minutes)

Type the following list.

```
          COMBINATION SIGNS AND SPECIAL CHARACTERS - LIST 3

   Cedilla                by using , (comma) under the small c as ç

   Dagger                 by using a capital I and - (hyphen) as ‡.

   Degrees                by using a small o slightly raised as 65°

   Double dagger          by using two capital I's, as ‡

   Equation               by using - (hyphen) and - (hyphen) as =

   Per mille (thousand)   by using three o's and / as °/oo

   Per cent               by using two o's and / as °/o

   Section sign           by using s and s as § or capital S's as §
```

Exercise 240 (Target time = 5 minutes)

Type the following material. Use combination characters if your machine is not fitted with any of the keys. Type in double-line spacing.

```
143 + 256 - 87 = 312              2' 6" + 5' 3" = 7' 9"

312 ÷ 3 = 104 x 7 = 728           7 14/25 x £19.25 = £145.53

75% of 1,000 = 750)               3 m x 3 m = 9 m²
50% of 1,000 = 500) Average = 50% -18 °C = 0 °F, 10 °C = 50 °F
25% of 1,000 = 250)               +12½% variation.  Accurate to 0.5%.
```

The omission of words in quoted matter (ellipsis)

Use full stops in groups of three (spaced or unspaced), to show the omission of a word or words at the beginning, in the middle or at the end of a passage of text. The three dots for the ellipsis may also be used for material such as advertisements where words are not actually omitted.

Exercise 241 (Target time = 5 minutes)

Type the following passage. Use spaced or unspaced dots consistently. Use double-line spacing.

```
The Avanti is the latest pocket computer with all the facilities you could wish
for ... powerful programming facilities ... plug-in peripherals ... links to
office-bound systems ... and a price tag from under £150.

As John Bird's review in Computer World Magazine said "... this is a powerful
yet compact, hand-held computer ... that no up-and-coming executive can afford
to be without ..." - can you afford to be without it?
```

One-line sentence drills

You should now try to increase your standard of accuracy and your typing speed, dividing your keyboard practice time about equally between the two goals. Set a left margin at 10 pica, 20 elite and type each individual line up to four times. Then copy each complete exercise once.

Exercise 30

```
A Precis is an abridged statement or summary of a document.
A Stockbroker is a middle man between a buyer and a seller.
A Jobber deals in stock through the medium of stockbrokers.
A Principal is the head or chief person in an organization.
A Free Port is one which levies no export or import duties.
Monopoly is the term applied to an exclusive right to sell.
```

Exercise 31

```
Discount is an allowance deducted from an invoice or retail price.
A Trade Discount is an allowance made to those who buy for resale.
Cash Discount is one allowed for the prompt payment of an account.
Obsolescence is the natural way in which assets diminish in value.
The Dollar is a currency unit equal in value to one hundred cents.
A Lunar Month is the period of time from one new moon to the next.
```

The tabulator

The operation of the tabulator quickly moves the carriage to any predetermined position. It can be set at required positions either by hand or by a special key provided for the purpose. When the tabulator bar or key is depressed, the carriage moves to the position for which the stop is set. To set a tabulator stop at 15, the space bar should be tapped five times from the left-hand margin point, when this is 10, and a stop set at this point. If a tabulator stop is set wrongly, or is no longer required, it can be 'cleared' by using the clearing key or lever provided.

Common-word paragraphs

The paragraphs contained in Exercises 32—41 consist of frequently occurring words, and provide copying and speed practice.

Indented paragraphs

These paragraphs are in the *indented style*, which means that the first line is indented five (six for elite) spaces from the left-hand margin. The use of the tabulator for this indentation is the quickest and most efficient way of starting new paragraphs.

Speed development

The paragraphs of each exercise can at first be copied, line for line, three times. Try to increase your speed. Finally, copy each paragraph as accurately and as quickly as possible for one minute. If you can complete any paragraph in less than one minute, start typing it again immediately after returning the carriage and depressing the tabulator. Keep your eyes on the copy all the time you are typing and do not erase, backspace or overtype.

13 Specialist work

Combination signs and special characters — Part 2

Combination signs are those formed by the typing of two or more characters in conjunction with one another. In this way the number of symbols that a machine will type is increased without adding to the number of keys. On a manual typewriter one character may be typed over another by holding the space bar down and successively striking the two characters. Another method, which avoids the uneven spacing caused by the first, is to strike one of the two signs and, after backspacing, to strike the second one over the first.

Special characters are those obtained by using a character already on the keyboard in a different way, or with a different purpose; or those added to or substituted for those normally found on a standard keyboard.

● For some combination signs where the original line has to be regained, the interliner should be used to allow the characters to be slightly raised (superior characters) or lowered (inferior characters) as required. On machines where half-line spacing is available, however, this will often provide the line variation required.

Exercise 238 (Target time = 10 minutes)

Type the following.

> COMBINATION SIGNS AND SPECIAL CHARACTERS - LIST 2
>
> Brace   by using opening (or closing) brackets
>   (   )
>   (   )
>
> Caret   by using the / (oblique stroke) and underscore
>   as /_
>
> Diaeresis (umlaut)   by using the quotation mark " and backspacer
>   as ü
>
> Division   by using : (colon), backspacer and - (hyphen)
>   as ÷
>
> Square brackets   by using the oblique stroke and underscore as
>   /_ _/. Use the backspace key; turn the
>   platen knob one full line space towards you
>   to type the underscore at the top of the
>   oblique stroke.

The plus sign cannot be satisfactorily obtained unless it is already provided on the keyboard. The dash and apostrophe can be combined, but the plus sign is generally better made with a matching colour pen in the absence of a special key.

Measuring your speed

An average of five strokes (character key or space bar) is allowed for a word. In the column on the right-hand side the numbers of strokes and words are shown. At the end of the minute, count the number of strokes you have typed (one for each character key or space bar operation), divide by five and enter the number of words typed in the right-hand margin. This figure is your gross speed in words per minute. Your teacher may suggest that you record your score for each test of one minute on a Progress Chart.

Proofreading

Check your work and circle all errors. You should have no more than two errors for each one-minute timing. If you do, intensive practice may be needed on letters on which you have made mistakes.

Note: The stroke-count, shown in the exercises below, includes the use of the shift key and carriage-return lever.

Exercise 32

Set the left margin stop at 10 pica, 18 elite and a
tabulator stop at 15 pica, 24 elite for the first line of each
paragraph

a
	Strokes
Language is part of our life, and we ought to try	50
to increase our command of it to extend our knowledge.	105
	(21 words)

b
The happiness of all depends upon each being reasonable	57
and kindly in outlook, undertaking responsibility as well as	118
demanding rights.	136
	(27 words)

Exercise 33

a
	Strokes
The uses of honey are unlimited. It can be included in	56
cakes, sweets, biscuits, beverages and savoury dishes and	114
many children enjoy it in sandwiches.	152
	(30 words)

b
Some children who have shown marked powers in their	52
early years grow up to be geniuses, while others develop	109
no further and make no names for themselves.	155
	(31 words)

c
Nowadays, it is possible for children to learn other	53
than through books alone and one of the most effective ways	113
of aiding education is by the use of toys.	156
	(31 words)

Exercise 34

a
	Strokes
A typist must always spell and punctuate correctly. A	54
business letter containing spelling or punctuation errors, or	112
both, creates a poor impression on the recipient.	162
	(32 words)

b
Comprehension is the name given to the process by which	56
we understand what we read or what we hear. The aim of	112
quicker reading is to increase the speed of comprehension.	171
	(34 words)

c
Always make sure that letters and enclosures for posting	57
are folded carefully and neatly. Take care not to fold a	115
document more than is necessary to fit it into its envelope.	176
	(35 words)

Type one copy of the following Agreement, in double-line spacing.

AN AGREEMENT made the   day of
One thousand nine hundred and
BETWEEN CHARLES WILLIAM BARNARD of 14 Anndale Road Mosley in
the City of Birmingham (hereinafter called 'the Manufacturer'
which expression shall where the context admits include the
Manufacturer's executors and administrators and assigns) of
the one part and THOMAS MUNDAY of 64 Ripon Road Nuneaton in
the County of Warwick (hereinafter called 'the Agent' which
expression shall where the context admits include the Agent's
executors and administrators and assigns or successors in
business as the case may be) of the other part ——————————

WHEREBY IT IS MUTUALLY AGREED as follows ———————————————

1. The Manufacturer grants to the Agent in consideration of the
    payment by the Agent of a non-returnable AGENCY FEE of One
    thousand pounds (the receipt whereof the Manufacturer hereby
    acknowledges) the sole and exclusive right to sell in the
    UNITED KINGDOM ONLY all items of sugar confectionery ordered
    for resale from the Manufacturer by the Agent on the following
    terms ——

    (a) The Manufacturer shall have the right to state the retail
    selling price of each separate item of confectionery ————————

    (b) The Agent shall be entitled to an allowance of forty per
    cent off the retail selling price of all confectionery ordered
    and invoiced and paid for under the terms of this Agreement —

2. The Agent hereby agrees that this AGREEMENT shall take effect
    immediately and that in the event of the aggregate total net
    value of all goods ordered and invoiced and paid for under the
    terms of this Agreement falling below one hundred thousand
    pounds in any one calendar year then this AGREEMENT may be
    terminated by the Manufacturer giving six months' written
    notice of termination of the aforesaid right ————————————————

    IN WITNESS whereof the parties hereto have hereunder set their
    hands the day and year hereinbefore written —————————————————

    SIGNED by the said   )
    CHARLES WILLIAM BARNARD)
    in the presence of   )

    SIGNED by the said   )
    THOMAS MUNDAY   )
    in the presence of   )

Exercise 35

a

Strokes

Quicker reading techniques have been developed because 55
of the increasing amount of written material which the 110
executive, the professional man and woman and the student 168
find they have to read. 192

(38 words)

b

Large numbers of people in the United States have been 55
trained to read at twice and even three times their original 117
speed without losing any of the comprehension of the material 178
which they are reading. 202

(40 words)

c

Because the weather is always with us it might quite 53
reasonably be expected that we should become so used to it 112
and all its changes that it would hold no special interest 171
for us. This is far from being the case. 213

(43 words)

Exercise 36

a

Strokes

A good letter is one which expresses clearly what has 54
to be said so that it is understood, and does so in a 108
favourable way. To this end, business letters should be 165
brief without being curt; friendly without being familiar. 224

(45 words)

b

There are few gardens where it would be impossible to 54
find a place for a lily pool. It is now possible to buy a 113
prefabricated shell for sinking into the garden. Some water 176
snails and other water insects will add to the interest. 231

(46 words)

c

It is astonishing how few people know how to speak well 56
on the telephone. Everybody uses it at some time or other, 116
yet very few of us attempt to train ourselves to the proper 176
use of this fine instrument. A low, clear voice is best. 234

(47 words)

Exercise 37

a

Strokes

There is a wonderful partnership between flowering 51
plants and insects. Flowers supply insects with food in the 112
form of nectar and pollen, whilst the insects, in turn, carry 174
the pollen from flower to flower and play their part in 230
fertilization. 245

(49 words)

b

Every office should have an efficient and reliable filing 58
system and a staff competent in the art of methodical filing 119
and indexing, so that correspondence and documents are kept 179
tidy, clear and always readily available for quick and easy 239
reference. 250

(50 words)

Type the following Will on A4 paper as an Engrossment. Type the endorsement on the back sheet.

<u>THIS IS</u>

T H E   L A S T   W I L L   A N D   T E S T A M E N T

of me

<u>CHARLES WILLIAM BARNARD</u> of 22 Richman Road Kettering in the County of Northampton which I made this   day of   One thousand nine hundred and _____

1   <u>I HEREBY REVOKE</u> all former wills and testamentary dispositions heretofore made by me and <u>DECLARE</u> this to be my last <u>WILL</u> _____

2   <u>I APPOINT</u> my wife Georgina Louise Barnard of 22 Richman Road Kettering aforesaid and John Brown of 27 Liverpool Crescent in the City of York to be the Executors of this my <u>WILL</u> _____

3   <u>I GIVE DEVISE AND BEQUEATH</u> all my estate and effects whatsoever and wheresoever <u>SUBJECT</u> to the payment thereout of my just debts funeral and testamentary expenses unto my Wife the said Georgina Louise Barnard absolutely _____

4   <u>I DIRECT</u> that my body shall be cremated and that the ashes shall be scattered wheresoever my Wife shall direct _____

<u>IN WITNESS</u> whereof I have hereunto set my hand _____

<u>SIGNED</u> by the said <u>CHARLES WILLIAM BARNARD</u>)
as and for his last Will and Testament   )   (Single spacing)
in our joint presence and by us in his :-   )

Legal work

Exercise 38

a
    In most countries, telegrams may be sent by telephone at any hour of the day or night but, as a permanent record is needed for the file, all details should be recorded in the same way as if the telegram were being sent direct from the post office counter.

Strokes
54
116
175
235
256
(51 words)

b
    A good secretary should know where information may be found, and she should familiarize herself with all the books of reference connected with her work so that she can check doubtful points instead of allowing them to slip into letters and documents in error.

54
115
174
236
260
(52 words)

Exercise 39

a
    Typists, shorthand typists and private secretaries are generally expected to know how to prepare stencils and master sheets and undertake the work of duplicating. It is important, therefore, for them to be conversant with the stencil, spirit and offset litho processes.

Strokes
55
117
181
243
271
(54 words)

b
    Modern typists should be able to type from recorded dictation, as well as from clear copy or shorthand notes. With recorded dictation, the typist is not present when her employer makes the recording; the tape, belt or disc is then passed on to her later for transcription.

52
110
170
231
273
(55 words)

Exercise 40

a
    Research is one of those things that are often talked about but little understood; yet it is, after all, nothing but looking forward to see in which direction industry may or may not go. Faith and patience are the two fundamentals on which all research organizations are built.

Strokes
54
113
175
235
279
(56 words)

b
    The Old Bailey, officially known as the Central Criminal Court, is the most important criminal court in England. It deals with all serious crimes in London and certain of the Home Counties and is housed in a fine modern building which stands on the site of the old Newgate Prison.

57
117
176
236
282
(56 words)

Exercise 41

a
    In modern offices, a number of the mailing operations have now been mechanized. There is a machine which collates up to eight enclosures, opens the envelope flap, inserts the enclosures, moistens the flap, seals the envelope, prints a postal impression on to the envelope and counts and stacks them ready for dispatch.

Strokes
54
115
176
236
295
320
(64 words)

b
    The typewriter has long been an indispensable piece of office equipment, and there are many styles and models from which to choose. They may be manually, electrically or electronically operated, heavy or portable. Some models are noiseless and some are even capable of typing braille, mathematical or technical symbols, or in foreign alphabets.

55
115
171
232
277
337
(67 words)

12 Legal work

It is important for all office typists to have an idea about displaying legal documents. However, in view of the specialist nature of legal work, when a legal document occurs in an exam paper, detailed instructions for the typist are usually given.

In theory there are three stages to producing a legal document:

- Draft — typed with wide margins, treble-line spacing.
- Fair copy — corrected draft in double-line spacing.
- Engrossment — final copy for signature, usually produced on a 'parchment substitute' material.

The engrossment is mostly typed in double-line spacing, without punctuation and with 'key' words and phrases in capitals or spaced capitals. Underlining is used and lines are inserted at the ends of clauses to prevent fraudulent additions. Except for dates of Acts of Parliament, house numbers and clause numbers, figures are not used.

Since the draft is only a rough copy, figures and abbreviations may be used. In practice, the draft or fair copy may be omitted from the 'sequence'. Nowadays, of course, word processors are extensively used in the production of legal documents and it is unlikely that drafts, fair copies and engrossments are produced as formerly. It is possible for standard paragraphs to be stored, recalled and 'personalised' so that documents are 'engrossed' without the two preparatory stages being necessary. If required for 'file purposes', photocopies can be made of engrossments or additional 'hard' copies can be 'run off'.

Endorsement

This is typed on the outside back sheet of a legal document so that it can be seen at a glance what the document is and who the 'parties' are.

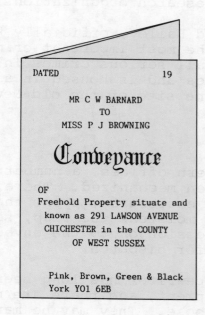

DATED   19

MR C W BARNARD
TO
MISS P J BROWNING

Conveyance

OF
Freehold Property situate and
known as 291 LAWSON AVENUE
CHICHESTER in the COUNTY
OF WEST SUSSEX

Pink, Brown, Green & Black
York YO1 6EB

The figure row; signs and symbols

New keys figures ¾ - (hyphen)

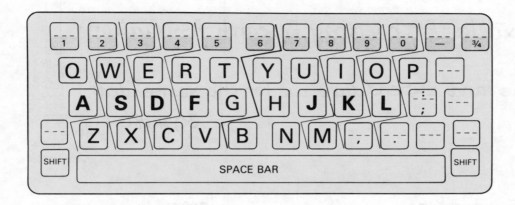

Exercise 42 and Exercise 43 introduce the ¾ sign, the - (hyphen) and all the figures. If your machine is not fitted with the 1 or O (zero) you can use the small letter l for numeral **1** and a capital letter **O** for **zero**. This is not advisable otherwise.

The new keys are introduced here in pairs, and this is a good way to read them in copy that contains three or more figures consecutively. The fingering for the top line of the keyboard is shown on the chart.

Before typing the following exercises you should compare the above chart with your typewriter to make certain that the various signs are in fact in the positions shown, and make allowances for any differences. If your machine does not have some of the signs, refer to page 24.

Exercise 42

Left margin	q1a p¾; q1a p¾; q1a p¾; q1a p¾; q1a p¾; q1a p¾;	Study the
20 pica	q2a p-; q2a p-; q2a p-; q2a p-; q2a p-; q2a p-;	chart
25 elite	w3s o0l w3s o0l w3s o0l w3s o0l w3s o0l w3s o0l	carefully
	q1a p¾; q2a p-; q1a p¾; q2a p-; q1a p¾; q2a p-;	before you
	q2a p-; w3s o0l q2a p-; w3s o0l q2a p-; w3s o0l	type
	w3s o0l q1a p¾; w3s o0l q1a p¾; w3s o0l q1a p¾;	

Exercise 43

Left margin	e4d i9k e4d i9k e4d i9k e4d i9k e4d i9k e4d i9k
20 pica	r5f u8j r5f u8j r5f u8j r5f u8j r5f u8j r5f u8j
25 elite	t6f u7j t6f u7j t6f u7j t6f u7j t6f u7j t6f u7j
	e4d i9k r5f u8j e4d i9k r5f u8j e4d i9k r5f u8j
	r5f u8j t6f u7j r5f u8j t6f u7j r5f u8j t6f u7j
	t6f u7j e4d i9k t6f u7j e4d i9k t6f u7j e4d i9k

On one sheet of A4 paper type the following.
This exercise formed part of a Stage III Examination set by the Royal Society of Arts.

Praxiteles Archaeology Research Association ⎫
⎬ caps centre & underscore

Income and Expenditure a/c for the year ended ⎫
30/4/86 ⎬ on one line centre & underscore

Expenditure	£	Income	£
Rent	435·00	Subscriptions	850·00
Cleaning	115·75	Dinner-Dance	212.73
Heating & Lighting	329·37	Sale of ties	125·50
Stationery	102·60	Sale of Lapel badges	98·00
Postages	227·55		
Printing	398·73	Donation from estate of R. Dodds	700·00
Ties (in stock)	153·50		
Lapel badges (in stock)	82·00	Cheese and Wine Party	219·63
Rates	243·15		
Excess of Income over Expenditure	117·85		
	2,205·50		2,205.50

I have examined the above Income & Expenditure a/c & confirm that it agrees with the Association's books

(Signed)   S Richards
Chartered Accountant

(in full) ⟶ Hon. Auditor

New keys signs and symbols

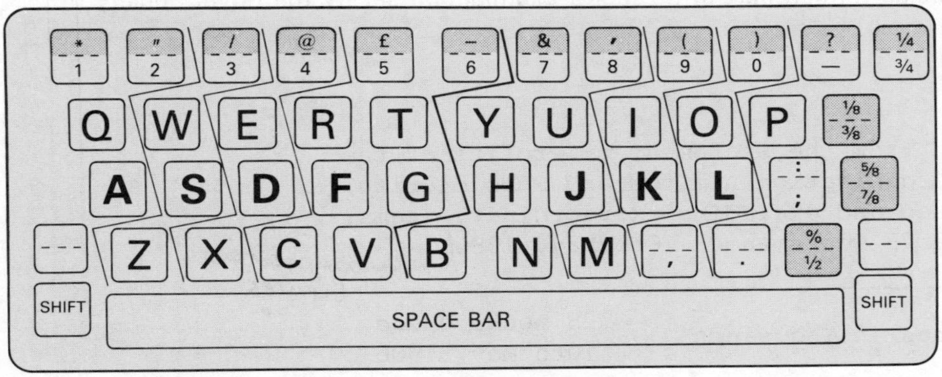

Exercise 44

Left margin 10 pica, 20 elite

£24 £36 £49 £63 £57 £82 £74 £85 (2) (9) (3) (8) (4) (7) (5) (6)
£1.00 £0.10 £234.56 6p 78p £1.06 £9.78 £2,755.01 £432.95 1p 83p
2 & 3 & 4 & 5 & 6 & 7 & 8 & 9 & 2 @ 3 @ 4 @ 5 @ 6 @ 7 @ 8 @ 9 @
'2' '3' '4' '5' "6" "7" "8" "9" 29¾ 53¼ 47¼ 86¾ 31¾ 72¼ ¾ @ ¼ @
1½% 2¼% 3¾% 4⅝% 5⅜% 6⅛% 7⅞% 8½% 10% 15% 20% 25% 30% 40% 50% 90%
2nd 3rd 4th 5th 6th 7th 8th 9th 1/32 5/16 47/80 £213,458,769.01

Exercise 45

Left margin 25 pica 35 elite

;p-; ;p-; ;p-; ;p-; ;p-; ;p-; ;-
;-; ;-; ;-; ;-; ;-; ;-; ;-; ;-;-
dumb-bell re-examine pre-eminent
self-evident non-party vice-dean
rolling-pin take-over life-saver

Exercise 46

Left margin 10 pica, 20 elite

Do not waste your time reading second-rate books.
Were all members of the team prepared to co-operate?
The fair-sized marquee held 1,345 exhibits at the show.
The 36 nightdresses are made of non-inflammable material.
Please re-cover the 24 armchairs and 12 settees by next week.
There has been a 10% increase in the use of self-service stores.

Open and full punctuation

In the open punctuation style all unnecessary punctuation is omitted. Full stops are omitted from abbreviations, and the whole abbreviation is typed as an unspaced group. In full punctuation the full stops are typed between the letters forming the abbreviation, as shown below. Either method is acceptable, but you must be consistent within each piece of typing. It is recommended that you use open punctuation style unless you are specifically requested to use the full punctuation style.

Exercise 234 (Target time = 15 minutes)

Type one copy of the following. Rule as shown. No additional ruling required. This exercise formed part of a Stage I Examination set by the Royal Society of Arts.

Extract from the Statement of Profits of the Tudor Organisation Limited and Subsidiaries, unaudited and excluding extraordinary items, for the 28 weeks ended 10th May, 1986/, *& with comparative figures*

£ figures in Thousands	28 weeks ended 10th May, 1986
	£
Turnover	130,547
Trading profit	6,106
Share of profits before taxation of Associated Companies	
Tudor Printing Group	31,299
Others	1,961
Dividends and interest	1,744
	41,110
Interest payable	9,514
Profit before taxation	31,596
Taxation based thereon (including United Kingdom Corporation Tax at 52%)	15,473
Profit after taxation	16,123

Add one more column, headed "28 weeks ended 10th May, 1985", & insert the figures in the order shown.

113,074
10,351
25,460
1,913
1,577
39,301
4,877
34,424
16,638
17,786

Note that the use of open punctuation style does not alter the punctuation of continuous text, where normal grammatical rules must still be applied.

Exercise 47

Type the examples below. Set a tab stop at 35 for the second column.

Full punctuation	Open punctuation
9.30 a.m.	9.30 am
0930 hrs.	0930 hrs
R.S.V.P.	RSVP
e.g.	eg
Mr. P. J. Roberts	Mr P J Roberts
12 December, 1988	12 December 1988
P.L.C. or p.l.c.	PLC or plc

DEGREES AND QUALIFICATIONS

Full stop (no space after each letter; comma and space after each group.	No space between the letters; one space after each group.
Mrs. R. Brown, M.A., B.Sc.	Mrs R Brown MA BSc

Time — the 24-hour clock

The 24-hour clock is now widely used. Times range from 0001 hrs (1 minute past midnight) to 2400 hrs (midnight).

Exercise 48

Type the following examples — set a left margin at 10, a tab stop at 24 for the second column, a tab stop at 40 for the third column and a tab stop at 52 for the fourth column.

EXAMPLES OF THE 24-HOUR CLOCK

Full punctuation		Open punctuation	
2.30 a.m.	0230 hrs.	2.30 am	0230 hrs
11.35 a.m.	1135 hrs.	11.35 am	1135 hrs
5.30 p.m.	1730 hrs.	5.30 pm	1730 hrs
9.15 p.m.	2115 hrs.	9.15 pm	2115 hrs

Any of these methods are acceptable provided you are consistent within one document.

Spacing

The most widely observed rules are:

No space
- Before or after a comma in figure work, eg, £2,600.
- Before or after the hyphen in compound words, eg, part-time.
- Before or after an apostrophe in one word, eg, boy's.
- After an opening bracket or before a closing bracket, eg, (noon).
- Before or after a full stop separating abbreviations, eg, B.B.C..

Exercise 232 (Target time = 5 minutes)

Type the following 'assets' section of a balance sheet.

HOME OWNERS' ASSOCIATION

Balance Sheet

as at 31 December 19--

ASSETS

		£	£
FIXED ASSETS			
	Equipment – at cost	2 700	
	Less provision for depreciation	900	1 800
INVESTMENTS			
	Newtown Building Society		16 749
CURRENT ASSETS			2 342
			20 891

Exercise 233 (Target time = 12 minutes)

Type the following as a list and insert the total at the foot of the column of figures. Insert leader dots. You need only type the £ sign before the first figure in the column and before any totals.

Management Expenses: Directors' Fees & Expenses £65,500; Staff Salaries £1,762,458; Staff Travelling Expenses £175,697; Remuneration of Auditors ~~£51,350~~ £52,390; Office Accommodation £1,108,429; Advertising £507,382; Commission & Agency Fees £1,672,780; Miscellaneous Expenses £29,275; Corporation Tax: £2,378,416

One space

- After a comma, colon, or semicolon.
- After an abbreviation within a sentence:

  We wrote to Messrs. Jackson & Co. yesterday.
  We wrote to Messrs Jackson & Co yesterday.

- After initial letters of names preceding surnames:

  Mr. J. P. Roberts or J. P. Roberts, Esq..
  Mr J P Brown or J P Robert Esq.

- Before and after the hyphen when it is used as a dash:

  He will arrive tonight — at least, I think so.

Two spaces

- After an exclamation mark, a question mark or a full stop at the end of a sentence.

Combination signs and special characters — Part 1

If your machine does not have some of these characters, read the general instructions on page 150, then follow the instructions for each sign.

Exercise 49

Type one copy of the following.

COMBINATION SIGNS AND SPECIAL CHARACTERS - LIST 1

SPECIAL CHARACTERS

Dash	by using one hyphen with a space before and after as -
Decimal point	by using . (full stop) as 16.53
Feet or Minutes	by using ' (apostrophe) as 10'
Fractions	by using $\frac{1}{4}$ and $\frac{7}{8}$, as $\frac{1}{4}\frac{7}{8}$, or 5 1/5 (known as a sloping fraction and now most widely used)
Inches or Seconds	by using " (quotation sign) as 6"
Minus	by using - (hyphen) as 10 - 5
Multiplication	by using small x as 5 x 8

COMBINATION SIGNS

Dollar	by using capital S, backspacer and / (solidus) as $
Exclamation mark	by using ' (apostrophe), backspacer and . (full stop) as !
Asterisk	by using a small x, backspacer and $-$ as $\overset{x}{-}$ raised above the line by using the interliner.

Oblique headings to columns

The only real advantage that can be claimed for oblique headings, as opposed to vertical headings, is that they are slightly more easily read without turning the sheet.

- The instructions on the previous page apply equally to this method of typing headings.
- When oblique headings are to be used, it is even more important that you should make certain that the platen on your typewriter is longer than the diagonal measurement of the sheet of paper you are using, eg the diagonal measurement of an A4 sheet is about 365 mm (nearly 14½ in) and you would require a 15-in (380-mm) platen. If your platen is not long enough you will need to fold the paper in order to type the oblique headings.

The calculation of the number of lines required for the boxes containing oblique headings can be made in the same way as for vertical headings. Type the main part of the table first, remove it from the machine and insert the ruling by hand, and then re-insert the sheet diagonally into the machine to type in the headings. You should always make the maximum use of tabulator stops and light pencil marks — to be erased later — for the starting point of the headings.

Exercise 231   (Target time = 15 minutes)

Type the following example and rule as shown.

GROUP II – TRAINING RESULTS

GROSS TYPING SPEED – WPM

Name	Letters	Memos	Reports	Meetings	Tables	Displays
S Abeoka	6.2	9.5	10.7	11.4	12.5	14.8
G Brown	4.5	6.2	8.8	9.1	10.5	12.6
G Charles	5.8	6.7	9.4	9.3	10.8	13.9
A Kaduna	5.5	5.9	5.6	7.8	9.6	11.5
G Malawi	4.3	4.8	5.3	5.8	8.6	10.5
S Obiola	6.1	7.6	7.8	6.9	9.3	9.1

Financial statements

- The style you choose for the typing of financial statements will depend a great deal on the nature of the material, the number and width of the columns and the overall depth.
- The copy you are given (either in an examination or in an office) will normally give you a guide to the layout required.
- The method of calculating the layout is the same as for any other tabulation.
- Where the task is given as a 2-sided column layout you must ensure that:

1 Headings are on the same horizontal line.
2 The totals are on the same horizontal line.

Note that a line may divide the 2 sides, or more space may be left.
- Proofreading is doubly important on documents of this nature. Check all figures carefully.

Typing measurements, weights and sums of money

Examples	Notes
MEASUREMENTS AND WEIGHTS	
2' 6"	No space before sign
or 2 ft 6 in	Space after number/before abbreviation
or 2 ft. 6 in.	or no space between, but be consistent within one document.
1.6 kg	
5 m x 2.6 m	One space either side of sign "x"
or	
167 + 43 - 21 = 189	
SUMS OF MONEY	
£6, $18 or £6.00, $18.00	If the amount comprises only the main unit of currency the two zeros may/may not be typed, but be consistent.
84p, 21c	If the amount comprises only a unit which is a division of the main currency - no space after number, no full stop after unit abbreviation.
£21.43, $16.20	Do not include the abbreviation for division of the main currency eg p, c
£4,700 or £3 900 £21,900 £23 800 £35,432,510 £47 998 022	When typed in columns, sums of money may be typed with or without a comma to indicate 'thousands'. Commas should be used to indicate 'thousands' when figures are typed in continuous text.

Note: Punctuation is never used in metric abbreviations.

Exercise 50

Type the examples above.

The use of words/figures in continuous matter

Within one document you should type figures as numbers or words. Either method, consistently used, is acceptable.
  In general:

- Do not begin a sentence with a figure.
- If a large number would be very long when written in words, type it in figures. For example 4,985 should be typed in figures, but 'five hundred' or 'seven million' may be typed in figures, where appropriate.
- Use figures for measurements and sums of money.
- Ordinal numbers (eg, first, second, third) are typed as words in continuous text. They may be typed as numbers if they are part of a company's name, as in '1st-Class Taxis', or in special cases such as '1st Prize', '50th Anniversary'.

Aim for consistency within the document.

Vertical headings to columns

When a table contains long headings, but the actual width of the detail in the columns themselves requires few spaces for each, you may have to use vertical headings as shown below so that the table is more compact.

- The main point for you to consider with this method is the depth the longest column heading will occupy when typed vertically. If there are several words in a heading, the depth should be reasonably controlled by typing these particular headings on more than one line.
- You must also remember to check that your typewriter platen will accommodate the sheet of paper when turned sideways; for a standard A4 sheet (298 mm, 11¾ in deep) you need at least a 12-in platen. If your platen is shorter than this, you will need to fold the paper to type in the vertical headings.
- This kind of table is generally more easily read if fully ruled.

EQUIPMENT ORDERED BY AGENTS

Agent	Displays	Showcases	Window Lettering	Showcards	Dummy Boxes	Posters	Notes
J Smithson	17	6	3	40	22	50	
W Andrews	28	9	12	17	12	36	
L Williamson	34	8	15	20	8	25	

To calculate the vertical space to be left for the headings

1. Count number of spaces in the longest heading, usually adding one space at either end (in the example, $11 + 2 = 13$).
2. **Pica** — 10 characters = 1" (6 vertical lines).
   So to convert pica to vertical lines:

   Heading $(13) \div 10 \times 6$
   $$\frac{13}{10} \times 6 = \frac{78}{10} \quad \text{(say) 8 lines.}$$

3. **Elite** — 12 characters = 1" (6 vertical lines).
   So to convert elite to vertical lines:
   $$\frac{13}{12} \times 6 = \frac{78}{12} \quad \text{(say) 7 lines.}$$

In some cases there may also be horizontal headings, and they should either be centred vertically in the space available or aligned with the bottom of the vertical headings — see 'Agent' and 'Notes' in the blocked-style example above. If you are using the centred style, these horizontal headings should also be centred horizontally across the width of their respective columns.

Exercise 230   (Target time = 10 minutes)

Type a copy of the above example in the blocked style.

Additional exercises on the figure row and fractions

The figures, signs, punctuation marks and fractions shown on the top portions of the keys — as well as the remaining fractions — are included in Exercises 50—53, and their positions on your machine should be carefully memorised and associated with the fingers that are used for striking them. The shift keys are used to type the miscellaneous characters, but when several successive capitals or upper-case characters are required, use the shift lock. A light touch on either shift key will release the shift lock. The spacing between the letters in the last two lines of Exercise 54 should be noted.

Set a left margin of 15 pica, 25 elite and repeat each exercise until you are completely familiar with the top row of the keyboard.

Exercise 51

'Ampersand' is the name given to the sign '&' for the word 'and'. It is used in the names of firms and companies, as: James Robinson & Co. Ltd.; and in postal addresses, as: 22 & 25 High Street, Findon, WORTHING, BN14 1YP.

Exercise 52

The nearest metric equivalent to 5' 3" would be 160 cm. The cost of 46 of these items @ 94p would be £43.24. One year's interest on £4,250 at $7\frac{1}{2}$% p.a. is £318.75. Have you seen my friend John? Have you spoken to him?

Exercise 53

The solidus sign '/' is used in typing fractions, as 18/37. Messrs. T. R. Williams & Co., Engineers, BARROW-IN-FURNESS. Many of the students - over 90% - had this well-known book. The current price of our £1 shares (fully paid) is £1.87. The asterisk sign '*' is used mainly as a reference mark.

Exercise 54

Our representative (Mr. A. Parker) will call on 8th August. I require 100 green plastic boxes measuring $9\frac{1}{8}$" x $6\frac{1}{4}$" x $3\frac{3}{8}$" in strong cardboard cartons measuring $9\frac{5}{8}$" x $6\frac{3}{4}$" x $3\frac{7}{8}$". The document was headed A B S T R A C T of T I T L E. The QUEEN'S BENCH DIVISION is part of the High Court.

Type the following table on A4 paper with the longer edge of the paper inserted into the typewriter first (landscape). Rule as shown. Use single-line spacing for the items in the table.

Table I – Analysis of clinician's questionnaire

| TEST | GRAND TOTAL | NORMALLY REQUESTED | | NOT NORMALLY REQUESTED | | | | |
| | | Total | Total Normal | Total | Total Normal | Total Expected | Total Diagnostic | Total Unexplained |
						ABNORMAL		
Glucose	2,069	200	200	1,811	1,630	25	33	123
Creatinine	2,071	307	223	1,764	1,620	73	12	59
Urea	2,068	1,342	1,139	726	702	5	4	15
Sodium	2,070	1,336	1,253	734	703	3	0	28
Potassium	2,067	1,332	1,181	735	701	3	3	28
Alk phosphatase	2,063	306	199	1,757	1,612	37	13	95
Bilirubin	2,068	237	177	1,831	1,722	18	9	82
Albumin	2,064	535	409	1,529	1,485	17	7	20
Globulin	2,070	539	409	1,531	1,363	44	10	114
Calcium	2,069	242	170	1,827	1,660	30	15	122
S.G.O.T.	2,064	161	109	1,903	1,869	16	4	14
Iron	2,065	136	57	1,929	1,482	192	72	183
Uric Acid	2,066	71	54	1,995	1,846	59	23	67
Cholesterol	2,059	229	182	1,830	1,705	29	13	83
TOTAL	31,439	7,236	5,926	24,203	22,307	576	225	1,095

Reproduced by kind permission of the Royal College of Physicians of London

Line-end division of words

A good typist aims to secure uniformity of margins on the right as well as the left, and it is sometimes necessary to break words, carrying over a part to the next line.

There are, however, certain rules to be followed, and these are for the most part based on common sense and the effect that the break will have on easy reading.

You may divide:

1   According to syllables: win-dow, men-tion, con-tact, com-muni-cate, cer-tifi-cate.
2   Before -ing: sell-ing, sing-ing; except where the final consonant of a word is doubled for the addition of -ing, in which case the division is made between the double consonant: get-ting, refer-ring.
3   Compound words, at the original hyphen: co-operate, glass-ware.
4   Words containing prefixes or suffixes, at the natural point of division, i.e. after the prefix or before the suffix: pre-cede, use-less, provided that two characters are not left standing alone.
5   Words containing a doubled consonant medially, between the two consonants: excel-lent, bril-liant.

Never divide:

1   In such a way that only one or two characters are left at the end of a line or carried forward to the next line: afraid, into.
2   Words of one syllable or their plurals: there, through, roses.
Note   An allowable departure from this rule occurs with the word 'children' which may be divided chil-dren.
3   Abbreviations or contractions: UNO, BCom.
4   Proper names: Larson, Northampton.
5   Numbers and sums of money: 56,843, £15.28.
6   The last word in a paragraph or on a page.
7   Words that already contain a hyphen, except at the point of the existing hyphen.
8   Numbers or courtesy titles from the words to which they refer: 8 months, Miss Brown.
9   Where the pronunciation of the word would be changed: mate-rial.

Margins

Throughout the world of business there is a variety of preference on the subject of margins in typewritten work. Wide margins are preferred by some, whilst others, possibly on grounds of economy, ask for narrow margins. No matter what style you use, always ensure that the use of a standard paper punch prior to filing will not obliterate any of the matter, most particularly if figures are involved.

Note:

● The right margin should never be wider than the left, and the work should generally be centred on the page.
● For general work, margins of 1" (25 mm) each side are usually acceptable.

After you have set a right-hand margin a bell on your typewriter will ring to warn you when the carriage is approaching the end of your line. The keyboard should lock when the carriage reaches the right-hand margin point. The use of the margin-release key will allow you to finish a word and you should remember that it is better to have a character or two extending into the margin than to break any of the rules for word division or to leave a line very short.

Many employers and examining authorities regard the achieving of a reasonably even right-hand margin as an unnecessary waste of time and instruct typists not to break words at ends of lines; but there are times when word division cannot be avoided.

Exercise 228 (Target time = 25 minutes)

Type the table shown below. Rule as shown.

Individual locks with different key combinations are normally available from stock.

SAFAMET SECURITY LOCKS AND FITTINGS

TYPE	FOR WOODEN WINDOWS			
	FOUR UNITS PER CARD		TWO UNITS PER CARD	
	REFERENCE NUMBER	PRICE ~~EACH~~ PER CARD	REFERENCE NUMBER	PRICE ~~EACH~~ PER CARD
Staylock	482001	£5·20	286114	£2·60
Sashlock	482004	£5·20	286402	£2·60
Dual Screw	482076	£8·00	286376	£4·15
Staybolt	483914	£6·00	289001	£3·15
Lockable Latch	483072	£16·25	288022	£8·50
TYPE	FOR METAL WINDOWS			
	~~FOUR~~ TWO UNITS PER CARD		ONE UNIT PER CARD	
	REF. NO.	PRICE PER CARD	REF. NO.	PRICE PER CARD
Patio Door Pushlock	221748	£15·00	100976	£7·95
Window Pushlock	223691	£14·95	144866	£6·90
Metal Window Lock	223482	£12·25	147904	£6·30
Transom Lock	224490	£4·20	149223	£2·40
Sliding Window Lock	226007	£3·90	149421	£6·80

ALL PRICES INCLUDE VAT

Examples of the appearance achieved *a* by breaking words correctly and *b* by not breaking words at all are given below.

a

    Men have for a long time shown a trend towards living together
in towns rather than spread over the countryside. Before the beginnings of agriculture men, of necessity, had to be dispersed over the
land, because hunting required a minimum of two square miles of territory to produce the food for one person. The agricultural revolution began to change all that. Because more food could be produced
in less area, people started to form primitive communities.

b

    Men have for a long time shown a trend towards living together
in towns rather than spread over the countryside. Before the
beginnings of agriculture men, of necessity, had to be dispersed over
the land, because hunting required a minimum of two square miles of
territory to produce the food for one person. The agricultural
revolution began to change all that. Because more food could be
produced in less area, people started to form primitive communities.

Exercise 55

Type the above paragraph yourself, using margins of 15—75 pica, 20—80 elite and making your own line-endings.

Exercise 56

Type the following words, indicating by a hyphen the best line-end division. Type in capitals any word that should not be divided.

lightning lightening plentiful splendour division programme statistics allotted maintain sometimes knowledge resignation children paragraph rule abroad ploughed Doncaster contraction troubling optician causes hundred movement partial Wilson intersperse folk-song pica appearance frustrate Australia fairly central £6,250,149

Exercise 227 (Target time = 25 minutes)

Display the following, paying careful attention to the instructions at the foot of the table. Rule as indicated.

TYPIST — Type columns containing 'reps' names in alphabetical order

SALES REPS — EXPENSES

Item	Expenses for month of January 19--				
	J Hart	T Twigg	H Lamb	R Page	Totals
Petrol & Oil	£175.98	£173.20	£176.45	£178.50	
Accommodation	£306.10	£388.10	£412.75	£449.80	
Meals	£98.75	£82.50	£101.45	£92.30	
Telephone	£55.40	£41.20	£49.32	£76.00	
Entertainment Expenses	£252.60	£244.95	£240.60	£375.66	
Totals					

Type a copy of the above info. Add the columns and rows and insert totals in the blank spaces.

3 Accuracy and speed development

Confidence and the power of concentration are essential to success in typewriting and will help you to reach a high speed.

Correct touch is an important factor and should be neither too heavy nor too light; if too heavy it naturally tends to reduce your speed. Correct and rapid operation of the carriage-return lever/key will also mean a saving of time.

Although the paragraphs given in Exercises 57-62 are very much shorter than the examination passages, they provide useful three- to five-minute practices. The remainder of the exercises in this section, with the exception of Exercises 63 and 64, each contain copying matter for up to ten minutes, depending upon your speed.

Accuracy and speed are both desirable, but accuracy is essential. Each exercise should be copied as quickly as possible two or three times, and then once or twice more for accuracy. Calculate your speed in the usual way. You should have no more than one error for each minute typed, plus one (eg, 3-minute timing = 3 + 1 therefore 4-error allowance). If you do not reach this standard, additional keyboard practice may be necessary on specific letters.

Exercise 57   Set the margin stops at 10 — 75 pica, 20 — 85 elite

a

	Strokes
Business firms throughout the world are now making an increasingly wide	72
use of machines to do work in the office, but this does not mean that there is	151
no place for skilled people in commercial offices. Machines may take care of the	233
routine work but there are many tasks which require tact and judgment, and	308
these will always have to be the responsibility of the office staff.	377
	(75 words)

b

An efficient electric dishwasher will clean, rinse and dry china, glass, pans	78
and cutlery to a brilliant sparkle in a very short time. It should work very quietly	162
and a popular size is one with a capacity in its stainless steel interior for twelve	247
place settings. It will be all the better if it can offer a choice of three or four fully	337
automatic programmes together with a built-in automatic self-regenerating	411
water softener.	427
	(85 words)

c

When choosing a motor-trailer caravan you will want one that is well within	76
the towing capability of your car. Most caravans have four berths because the	155
two-berth versions usually cost more since additional furniture items replace	233
the beds. You should check that there is enough sensibly planned storage space	313
and really make sure that the caravan will comply with all your requirements.	391
Then you will experience the real joy of independence on caravan holidays.	466
	(93 words)

Type the following on one sheet of A4 using single-line spacing for the introductory paragraphs. This exercise formed part of a Stage II Examination set by the Royal Society of Arts.

Closed caps. A Guide to Hardwoods

unless a special micro-porous paint is used

These timbers are used for their interesting textures, attractive colours and complex grain patterns. Hardwoods are also used as thin veneers over man-made boards to give the appearance of solid wood, but with improved stability and a considerable reduction in cost.

para. // Hardwoods are usually varnished, oiled, waxed or polished, but can also be painted. However, if used outside hardwoods should not be painted.

close up Although most hardwoods really are harder than soft woods, the different species vary in strength and resistance to weathering. The *table* ~~chart~~ below shows their properties.

Typist Pl. re-arrange the table so that the woods are in alphabetical order.

Hardwood	Properties (see notes)			
	Shade	Grain	Durability	Density
AFRORMOSIA	1	3	1	1
MAHOGANY	1	3	2	3
BEECH	2	3	3	1
ELM	2	1	3	2
OAK	2	2	1	1
TEAK	2	3	1	1
WALNUT	2	2	2	1
ASH	3	3	3	1
SYCAMORE	3	2	3	2

NOTES

Shade - Varies from dark to light; 3 = lightest.

Grain - Varies from straight to swirling; 3 = straightest.

trs. ⌐ Density - Varies greatly; 3 = least dense.

  ⌐ Durability - Preservative treatment is necessary for timbers used outside; 3 = least durable.

Exercise 58

a

Home dressmaking is a very popular hobby. It is highly creative, good fun 75
and very rewarding. There are many sewing aids and every gadget imaginable 150
designed to make the work easier, and the domestic sewing machines available 227
today can produce the most exciting effects in a very few minutes. There is the 308
right sewing thread for every type of fabric, both in natural and man-made 383
fibres, and for success it is important to match the thread with the fabric so 460
that when laundered and ironed they will shrink and stretch together. 531

(106 words)

b

There are two ways of doing a fly-cruise. You could go to, say, New York by 77
sea, spending some glorious days afloat, generally unwinding and gradually 152
getting ready for a holiday in the United States, at the end of which time you 231
would return by air. On the other hand, if you prefer to have a very active, 309
sight-seeing time in America first, it is best to fly there, take the hectic holiday 394
and then relax on the return journey by sea. Either way, you will enjoy all the 475
pampered luxury of a sea cruise which is tantamount to having a second holiday. 555

(111 words)

Exercise 59

a

Strokes

There is a constant challenge in the problems of old age. The old folk often 78
know but are rarely asked. They are sometimes scorned by the young as well as 157
by Nature. Every year more people live longer and we are faced with the realiza- 239
tion that as Mother Earth ages so do her inhabitants. It is, therefore, most 317
important that in extending the human being's life span, we make the added years 412
worth living and in this respect we should perhaps listen more carefully to our 480
elders. Knowledge can always be obtained easily from textbooks but wisdom— 556
a much rarer commodity—comes only with age. 600

(120 words)

b

New York is the largest city in the United States. Greater New York consists 78
of five boroughs: Manhattan, which occupies Manhattan Island, is the heart of 156
the City; Brooklyn is on the east across the East River; Queens adjoins Brooklyn 237
on the north-east; Richmond occupies Staten Island and the Bronx is the resi- 315
dential and business section north of the Harlem River. New York is a city of 394
contrasts and infinite variety. There are massive skyscraper buildings and 470
cosmopolitan crowds making it the most exciting city in the world. There is so 548
much to do and so much to see as part of the dynamic expression of the whole of 628
American Civilization. 651

(130 words)

Exercise 224 (Target time = 10 minutes)

Type the following table on A4 paper. Rule as shown. This exercise formed part of a Stage III Examination set by the Royal Society of Arts.

FAMILY RELIEF NURSING SERVICE

Queensland Lane Fishponds BRISTOL BS16 7LK

Telephone (0272) 693021

CURRENT RATES FOR PRIVATE CASES

	RELIEF NURSING SERVICE		SPECIAL TREATMENT RATE		AUXILIARY SERVICES	
	Registered General Nurse	Enrolled Nurse (General)	Registered General Nurse	Enrolled Nurse (General)	Auxiliary	Special Treatment Rate
Salary	£2.70	£2.20	£3.20	£2.70	£1.95	£2.45
Service Fee	75p	75p	90p	90p	75p	80p
Total Hourly Rate	£3.45	£2.95	£4.10	£3.60	£2.70	£3.25

1 August 1985

Exercise 225

Type the following table. Rule as indicated.

CANCER RESEARCH

Site of Cancer	3-year Survival Rate when diagnosed		Site of Cancer	3-yr. Survival Rate when diagnosed	
	1949	1969		1949	1969
Bladder	48%	62%	Larynx	41%	54%
Bone	34%	41%	Leukaemia	0%	15%
Brain	28%	37%	Liver	7%	13%
Colon	36%	50%	Lung	6%	11%
Eye	77%	84%	Mouth	41%	51%
Kidney	31%	44%	Nose	30%	47%

Exercise 60

	Strokes
One of the most important books on a person's bookshelf is a dictionary.	72
It is necessary for immediate reference to the spelling and/or meaning of unusual	154
words, a practice which aids the development of vocabulary.	214
In the preface there is usually a list of the abbreviations used in the explanation	300
of the words. Apart from the meaning of a word, information is given about its	380
function (whether it is a noun, adjective, verb, etc.), the origin of the word, if	464
that is known, and its idiomatic or colloquial use, if any.	524
After the words one can often find a list of abbreviations in common use,	599
together with a guide to the pronunciation of proper names.	659

(RSA I) (132 words)

Exercise 61

	Strokes
Swimming pools are no longer the expensive item that they used to be;	70
nowadays it is possible for anyone to own a garden pool provided he has the	146
space. Because these cheaper pools are 'freestanding' pools, they do not require	228
expensive excavations. They can be erected on any level site by unskilled people.	310
Most pools can be purchased in a variety of sizes and depths and are delivered	390
in sections of interlocking panels. Inside the box-like structure is suspended a	472
heavy-duty polythene lining which is subsequently held in place by a wooden	548
capping.	557
Numerous swimming pool accessories are available for purchase: filter units,	634
heating units, steps, shelters with changing rooms – a must for most owners,	709
who usually find themselves besieged by friends whenever the sun shines.	781

(RSA I) (156 words)

Exercise 62

	Strokes
Of all the remarkable changes that took place in the nineteenth century,	73
perhaps none was more notable and unexpected than the transformation of	145
Japan. In 1850 it was an obscure Asiatic country, which for two hundred years	224
had shut itself up tightly from the rest of the world. Foreigners were not allowed	308
to enter the kingdom, and subjects were forbidden to leave under penalty of	384
death.	391
Then suddenly came the awakening. In July 1853 Commodore Matthew C.	461
Perry appeared off the coast with a squadron of ships of the United States	536
Navy, sent to induce Japan to enter into trade relations with the nations of the	617
West. After some time spent in negotiations a treaty of friendship was signed	696
in February 1854 by which Japan agreed to open certain ports to American	769
vessels.	777
European countries, which for some time had been seeking to open up Japan,	853
now followed this lead. After a few years of hesitation Japan unlocked the doors	935
of its Empire, and began rapidly to adopt Western civilization.	999

(RSA II) (200 words)

Rule as indicated. Except for column headings use double (or 1½) line spacing throughout. Re-arrange in alphabetical order according to course subject, beginning with 'About Antiques'. This exercise formed part of a Stage II Typewriting Examination set by the Royal Society of Arts.

LEISURE CLASSES FOR ALL THE FAMILY

Course	Day	Centre	Fee	
			Resident in Borough	Under 18
Home Repairs	Mon	J	£ 6.00	£ 3.00
Woodcarving	Wed	WM	8.00	4.00
About Antiques	Thur	WM	6.00	3.00
Vegan Cookery	Fri	J	6.00	3.00
Patchwork	Wed	J	9.00	4.50
Popmobility	Tue	HM	6.00	3.00
Car { Maintenance { Repair	Wed	J	12.00	6.00
Batik	Fri	WM	10.00	5.00
Yoga (1) elementary	Thur	MC	5.00	2.50
(2) intermediate	Thur	J	5.00	2.50

ALL CLASSES RUN FROM 7-9 PM

Non-resident in Borough: add £5 to fee for residents

Centres: J = Johnson Hall
HM = Highams Park
WM = William Morris House
MC = Mersey College

Typist - align = signs under each other

Typist - to be added to table, in alphabetical order -
Aerobics   Fri   J   6.00   3.00

Control drills

These exercises should be used regularly throughout your course in order to check your speed. Type each line as accurately as possible three times before going on to the next. Your teacher may control the rates by indicating when the carriage is to be returned, and may call 'carriage return' at intervals of 20, 15 or 12 seconds. The speed reached for each line is shown beside each section.

Your practice on these drills should not exceed ten minutes at any one time. Try to repeat the drill several times a week.

Exercise 63

a

Shyness is often a phase that will pass.
Millions of people are indoor gardeners.
The nursing profession needs new skills.

40-stroke lines:
20" = 24 wpm
15" = 32 wpm

b

Belgium's farmland is intensively cultivated.
Freesias are as easy to grow as indoor bulbs.
Soda bread is a traditional bread of Ireland.

45-stroke lines:
20" = 27 wpm
15" = 36 wpm

c

Short advertisements on television increase sales.
Brussels is the headquarters of the Common Market.
Tartans are widely used in the textile industries.

50-stroke lines:
20" = 30 wpm
15" = 40 wpm

Exercise 64

a

Our nails grow faster in summer than they do in winter.
The amount of rest needed varies from person to person.
Holland and Belgium are often called the Low Countries.
The calorific value of crash diets is usually very low.

55-stroke lines:
20" = 33 wpm
15" = 44 wpm

b

A Japanese bride can hire any kind of dress for her wedding.
Tunisia is a holiday resort with a thousand-mile-long beach.
The modern domestic freezer is a great help in housekeeping.
Windmills form a traditional feature of the Dutch landscape.

60-stroke lines:
15" = 48 wpm
12" = 60 wpm

c

It is often prudent to undertake correspondence courses of study.
Wine and cheese parties give plenty of scope for the imagination.
There is a very wide range of exciting plants in outdoor gardens.
Malham Tarn in North Yorkshire is a genuine relic of the Ice Age.

65-stroke lines:
15" = 52 wpm
12" = 65 wpm

d

Controlled deep breathing is often a great aid to complete relaxation.
Sir Christopher Cockerell invented the hovercraft as we know it today.
Benjamin Law invented machinery for processing woollen waste and rags.
The food value of oysters is supreme because of their mineral content.

70-stroke lines:
15" = 56 wpm
12" = 70 wpm

Type the following table on plain paper. Rule only where indicated.
This exercise formed part of a Stage II Typewriting Examination set by the Royal
Society of Arts.

PRAXITELES WINES

Special offers for April

Name of Wine	Year	Comments	Price	
			Per bottle	Per dozen
Château d'Aigueville	1982	A consistently good wine which has been a favourite with our customers for a number of years	£ 3.15	£ 34.65
Mainzer Domherr	1983	A lasting, pleasant fruity flavour	3.75	41.25
Château Cissac	1979	Fine, full-bodied and satisfying. Drink now or keep for a few years	3.15	34.65
Serriger Herrenburg	1983	Dry with a subtle elegance and charm	4.35	47.85
Montagny	1982	Dry, fruity and full-bodied. Ideal with fish and chicken dishes	6.55	72.00
Château de la Bretesche	1983	Fairly dry with an appetising fresh flavour	3.75	41.25

Typist: Please arrange the wines in order of year, starting with the earliest. When there is more than one for the same year, please arrange them in alphabetical order.

Exercise 65

In the autumn of 1970 there were so many champagne grapes they did not	71
know what to do with them. Pickers ran short of baskets. Presses could not keep	153
up. To store the fantastic flood of juice, wine firms turned desperately to tank	235
barges, abandoned water towers, even swimming pools.	288
That was the scene I watched in the French champagne country during the	361
grape harvest of 1970—the great, the incredible, the fabulous year that broke	438
all records in the long history of the world's most glamorous wine. 'Never since	521
Noah,' exulted one young Frenchman, 'has there been such a flood.'	588
This fantastic harvest resulted in about 30 million gallons of champagne—	662
enough to fill 64 Olympic swimming pools or 170 million bottles, and to draw	739
from pockets around the world more than £400 million. Not bad for a business	817
based on bubbles.	835
But what bubbles! They transform champagne from a mere beverage into a	908
mood, a myth, a miracle. They confer the gift of gaiety—'like the laugh of a	986
pretty girl', the French say—and make champagne just right for celebrating	1061
a wedding or a promotion, for christening your ship or your son. More than 100	1143
million bottles of champagne were sold—double the figure of only ten years	1216
ago. (RSA III)	1221

(244 words)

Exercise 66

New York, largest city in the United States, lies on the Atlantic Coast at the	79
mouth of the Hudson River. It comprises 5 boroughs sprawling over 300 square	157
miles, with 8 million residents. Within the 13-mile length and 2½-mile breadth	237
of the Island of Manhattan is the frenzied world of advertising and journalism,	317
the diplomatic meeting place of world leaders, and Lincoln Centre's million-	393
dollar marble complex of culture and entertainment.	445
Bringing life and action to the city are Wall Street, synonymous with high	521
finance and the thrill of the stock market; Greenwich Village, where the avant-	601
garde artistic life flourishes; Park Avenue, the broad, flower-trimmed boulevard	682
of luxury apartments and modern skyscrapers; Seventh Avenue, notable for	755
its fashion industry; Fifth Avenue, reputed shopping thoroughfare; and	826
Broadway, a renowned theatrical centre.	866
Since 1626, when the first boatload of settlers arrived from the Netherlands,	946
people from every land have continued to pour into the city adding the colour	1021
and flavour of their homeland. New York has its own Chinatown, Little Italy,	1098
German quarter, Greek, Czech and other sections. It is a vibrant city with a	1176
many-faceted personality welcoming 16 million visitors annually from all parts	1255
of the world. (RSA III)	1269

(254 words)

VEHICLES (Single Fares)
(including cars, caravans and baggage trailers, motorised caravans and minibuses)

	Southampton to Lisbon £	Southampton to Tangier £
Overall length not exceeding 8 feet	108	111
Overall length exceeding 8 feet, not exceeding 18 feet and height not exceeding 8 feet	~~116~~ ~~116~~ 120	123
Vehicles exceeding 8 feet in height and up to 18 feet in length	122	130
Motorcycles and scooters	64	66
Pedal cycles	21	22

Exercise 221 (Target time = 15 minutes)

Type one copy of the following table on plain paper. This exercise formed part of a Stage II Examination set by the Royal Society of Arts.

Typist Keep abbreviation of days and months

COURSES	1986 DAYS/DATES	SESSIONS	~~TIME~~
uc Parent and baby	Mon Sept 22 – Oct 20) Wed Sept 24 – Oct 22)	10 (2 x 5)	~~1730 – 1800~~
Female Fitness	Tues Sept 23 – Nov 25	10	~~1730 – 1800~~
Male Fitness	Fri Sept 26 – Nov 28	10	"
Children's Learn to Swim	Tues " 23 – " 25	10	~~1600 – 1630~~
Senior Citizens' Recreation Hour	Wed " 24 – " 26	10	~~1600 – 1700~~
Ladies' Recreation	Thurs " 25 – " 27	10	~~1730 – 1800~~
Family Recreation – Parents plus (own) under 11s	Sun " 28 – " 30	10	~~0900 – 0945~~
Children's Stroke Improvement	Thurs Sept 25 – Nov 27	10	~~1600 – 1630~~

Exercise 67

Men have for a long time shown a trend towards living together in towns rather than spread over the countryside. Before the beginnings of agriculture men, of necessity, had to be dispersed over the land, because hunting required a minimum of two square miles of territory to produce the food for one person. The agricultural revolution began to change all that. Because more food could be produced in less area, people started to form primitive communities.

The growth of cities continues today, but at an increasing rate. Between 1950 and 1960, the populations of cities in the highly-developed countries increased by twenty-five per cent, and in the less developed countries by fifty-five per cent. In countries like Britain and the United States, seventy per cent or more of the population live in cities or their suburbs. In Africa, Nairobi, the capital of Kenya, has a population of half a million people and is growing at the rate of seven per cent per year; Lagos, the capital of Nigeria, is growing at the rate of fourteen per cent per year.

Young people in particular are attracted to the opportunities for both work and enjoyment in cities. Even though they may have to live in a bedsitter in London, or a migrant settlement in Peru, they have often burnt their bridges and usually have no desire to return to a rural life. (LCCI Elem)

(268 words)

Strokes
72
151
230
307
386
457
537
617
702
778
863
943
1025
1053
1130
1207
1284
1338

Exercise 68

The would-be bee keeper must understand something of the life and the habits of the honey bee. This does not imply laborious research into the insect's natural history; all that is required is a fair knowledge of how a colony works and lives.

The honey bee (*Apis mellifica*) differs in one important respect from the bumble bee and the various other kinds indigenous to this country. They are social insects, living in large colonies and working for the common good. Most of the other types are solitary or non-gregarious. It is this social habit that makes the honey bee so valuable an insect. By reason of their numbers they are enabled to maintain a winter temperature in the hive which is high enough to ensure their survival in any normal winter. Were the numbers of any one colony to be greatly reduced, it is very doubtful if they could come through unscathed, for the smaller the number of bees in a hive the lower the temperature will be, and the insects are extremely susceptible to cold.

There are three different classes of bee in a colony: the Queen, the worker, and the drone. So distinct are these that they are frequently regarded as three sexes, though this is not correct from the scientific standpoint. The Queen is the only fully-developed female. She is the head of the colony and the mother of every bee in the hive. (RSA III)

(269 words)

Strokes
70
152
235
242
316
392
472
559
641
717
796
875
954
1001
1079
1160
1240
1322
1345

To type/rule vertical lines

1 It is advisable to leave an odd number of spaces between columns.
2 Type the first horizontal line. The beginning and end of this line will be the outer vertical lines.
3 Move to the first tab stop. If there are 3 spaces between columns, backspace 2 (backspace 3 for 5 spaces) to get to the centre of the column. Make a pencil mark at this point.
4 Do the same as in 3 above for the centre of each column.
5 After you type the horizontal line at the bottom of the table, put the same pencil marks along this line.
6 Remove the paper and rule the vertical lines using either the underscore or a matching pen.

Exercise 219   (Target time = 10 minutes)

Type the following example. Rule as shown.

Class	Enrolments		Percentages of enrolments under 21	
	Male	Female	Male	Female
Accountancy	12	8	40	80
Computing	10	10	60	50
Marketing	6	14	90	70

Exercise 220   (Target time = 30 minutes)

Type the following two tables on one sheet of paper, making sure that they are the same width. Rule neatly either in ink or on the typewriter. This exercise formed part of an Elementary Examination set by the London Chamber of Commerce and Industry.

FARES PER BERTH, INCLUDING MEALS → *Centre*   *TYPIST: Both tables to be same WIDTH*

	Southampton to Lisbon Single	Southampton to Tangier Single
	£	£
De luxe cabins (twin-bedded)		
De luxe B deck with bath	~~160~~ 170	~~170~~ 180
De luxe bridge deck (shower)	~~150~~ 160	~~165~~ 175
De luxe B deck (shower)	~~150~~ 160	~~165~~ 175
Two-berth cabins		
B deck inside	~~145~~ 150	~~158~~ 163
C deck outside	~~145~~ 150	~~158~~ 163
C deck inside	~~140~~ 145	~~152~~ 157
D deck outside	~~140~~ 145	~~152~~ 157
E deck outside	~~136~~ 139	~~145~~ 150

Infants under three */years* are carried free if separate berth is not required. All other children under twelve */years* travel at half fare.

Exercise 69

	Strokes
Elephants have been a part of man's life in Africa since neolithic times. In	77
those days painters adorned rock faces throughout Africa with the representations	157
of these beasts and their mammoth ancestors. Later, Aristotle was a keen	231
observer of the capture and training of elephants, and himself dissected a	306
specimen, recording that its liver was four times as large as that of an ox.	382
The elephant's size—it can reach 13 feet tall—was obviously one of the reasons	462
for its popularity with the warriors of old. The Seleucid hordes doing battle	541
with Ptolemy Philadelphus, and the Romans who fell to Hannibal, doubtless	613
quaked at the sight of a phalanx of the largest land mammals charging towards	691
them with heads down and ears flapping.	729
These massive beasts of war and burden are also beset with ills such as bile	807
stones, sunstroke, varicose veins and heart attacks, and they sometimes display	886
a touching tendency for the young to help the very old by acting as protective	965
attendants.	977
The ivory trade was one of the main reasons for the drastic reduction in	1051
numbers of elephants. To counteract this, African governments set up national	1130
parks, sanctuaries and controlled zones. Here the elephants settled, giving up	1210
their migratory way of life—they have been known to travel distances of 300	1226
to 400 miles at a speed of about 10 miles an hour. (RSA III)	1337
	(267 words)

Exercise 70

	Strokes
Portugal is a country which can only be visited satisfactorily with a car. The	80
picturesque spots, the quaint towns and the beautiful sights are scattered just	160
about everywhere, and as the distances between the tourist centres are short the	241
motorist is able to stop frequently. The main roads are of a high standard,	318
although flat or dead straight stretches are rare.	369
Portugal is a highly civilized country whose people will make the traveller	445
very welcome. The best season for a car trip is the spring. As Portugal is the	526
kingdom of flowers, spring is the time when the country is at its most beautiful.	608
In autumn the light is wonderfully soft and fruit abounds, but by this time much	689
of the countryside has been scorched by the fierce summer sun. In the chief	764
towns and the popular bathing resorts first-class hotels are to be found; in	840
the less important places hotels are rather modest, but the authorities have	917
established in the most picturesque spots pousadas, model inns furnished in the	997
local style, where the tourist finds pleasant accommodation and good meals.	1073
The car ferry to Portugal involves two full days at sea and so avoids the long	1152
and tiring journey across France and Spain. The sea approach to Lisbon passes	1231
the elegant resorts of Cascais and Estoril before the ship ties up in the shadow of	1315
the splendid suspension bridge spanning the River Tagus. There is a choice of	1394
shore excursions with an English-speaking guide. (LCCI Elem)	1443
	(289 words)

Multiple line column headings (column headings of more than one line)

- Use blocked or centred display.
- Headings should be aligned at the top of each column, the bottom of each column or centre each in the total space allocated, but be consistent.

Sub-divided headings

- Use either blocked or centred style for each column.
- You *must* be consistent within the whole tabulation.

Exercise 218 (Target time = 10 minutes)

Type the following example.

Class	Enrolments		Percentages of enrolments under 21	
	Male	Female	Male	Female
Accountancy	12	8	40	80
Computing	10	10	60	50
Marketing	6	14	90	70

Ruling a table

- You may be asked to rule a table, or you may just feel that ruling would make the table clearer.
- The table may have only horizontal ruling, or it may have both horizontal and vertical lines.
- Use the underscore for the horizontal lines.
- Draw the vertical lines with a matching coloured pen to rule the complete table after the paper has been removed from the machine.
- When using vertical ruling, the main heading is not usually included in the ruled sections.
- Make sure that joins are made neatly, not overlapping.

To type horizontal lines

1 It is advisable to leave additional space where ruling is to be inserted, to give a more open appearance.
2 Set tab stops and calculate vertical starting point in the usual way. (See page 92.)
3 Move to the last tab stop, tap the space bar once for each character in the longest line, *plus* 2 — set the right margin.
4 Type the main heading.
5 Turn up once (or however many spaces needed) — this is the position of the first horizontal line — return the carriage to the left margin.
6 Press the margin release key and backspace 2 — this is the starting point for all horizontal lines.
7 Type the horizontal line using the underscore, finish at the right margin.
8 Remember that to leave 1 clear space above the next line of type you will need to turn up 2 spaces.

Exercise 71

	Strokes

The ceremony attending the laying of a foundation stone has been evolved | 73
by tradition without being governed by any specific ritual and may be adapted | 151
to suit particular circumstances. The position of the stone should be determined | 233
as soon as possible after the contract has been let. By custom it should be in the | 317
north-east corner of the building, but if this is not suitable, some prominent | 396
position should be chosen where it will be seen by people passing or entering the | 478
building. | 488

Shortly before the occasion, the stone should be in position on the handling | 566
equipment, and the foreman mason should have all the implements ready, | 637
together with some fine mortar, free from grit. The tools required will be a | 715
clean trowel, mallet, level and plumb line. It is usual for the person performing | 797
the ceremony to be given a presentation case containing a trowel, perhaps made | 875
in silver, and a mallet, and these implements should actually be used. | 945

On the day of the ceremony the employer will make a short speech describing | 1022
the purpose of the building to be erected. He will ask the invited person to lay | 1104
the stone, and the trowel and mallet will be presented to him. The foreman | 1180
mason will then spread the mortar evenly on the bed. This operation will be | 1257
completed with the presentation trowel, and the stone will be slowly lowered | 1334
into position. The guest will then tap the top two or three times and declare the | 1417
stone to be well and truly laid. (LCCI Elem) | 1449

(290 words)

Exercise 72

	Strokes

A basic characteristic of all consumers, as far as clothes are concerned, is their | 83
varying degree of interest in the subject. Few are completely uninterested. Often | 167
this interest is part of their overall way of life and sometimes is more specifically | 253
linked with their occupation. | 283

It is a characteristic which appears to change slowly—if at all—except when | 359
there is a substantial change in the way of life. One of the major changes here | 440
takes place, for women, on marriage or, even more significantly, on leaving work | 521
and starting a family. Equally a dramatic change can take place when a woman | 598
returns to work having brought up a family. In this case, her going to work may | 679
demand a greater interest in clothes and a larger wardrobe, and at the same time, | 761
provide the money for their purchase. | 799

Adolescents, other than students, tend to take a keen interest in clothes, and | 879
this is related to their way of life. A large proportion of their leisure time is spent | 967
outside their home and in the company of others and clothes are important to | 1044
them in this situation. Clearly from the point of view of forecasting future | 1122
demand for clothing, it is important to know the extent to which this interest of | 1204
adolescents is going to be maintained into later life. This is an important topic | 1287
for more detailed investigation, but the work so far undertaken suggests that | 1364
some of this interest will decrease. This results, again, from a change in the | 1444
way of life. (LCCI Inter) | 1457

(291 words)

11 Tabulation (Part 2)

This section contains more advanced tasks, many involving column sub-headings. The example below shows how to use the centred style, where columns are centred under the column headings (see pages 91 and 92).

Centred style (columns centred under column headings)

```
                    EVENING CLASSES


                Classes held on Monday


            Subject    Time    Room

            Art        1400 hrs    62
            Craft      1800 hrs     3
            Yoga       1800 hrs    14
```

1 Follow steps 1 to 2 *e* on page 92.
2 To centre columns under headings:

a Set the tab stops for the longest line in each column. This may be a line in the column or the column heading itself, so you may need to re-calculate for the column *or* the heading, whichever is shorter.

b Consider each column separately. In the first column above:

   i   The heading is the longest line, therefore, this is where the tab stop is set.
   ii Centre the longest line in the *column* under the heading and start all lines at this point.
   iii As the lines in the example are short lines, it is easier to count the characters in both the heading and the column, then subtract the smaller (Craft = 5) from the larger (Subject = 7), divide by 2 and tap the space bar once to begin the column.
   iv For longer lines the arithmetic or backspacing method of centring can be used. The principle is the same — centring one item (eg Craft) across the available space (Subject).

c The tab stop was originally calculated for the longest line. You may type the headings on the original tab stops, re-set the tab stops and type the columns. Alternatively you can re-set the tab stops for the columns, but you must remember to use the backspace or space bar to type the headings.

As this style is time-consuming, you should use it only where you are instructed to do so.

Exercise 217   (Target time = 5 minutes)

Type the example above.

Exercise 73

In the last ten years about forty thousand robots have been made. These deaf and dumb machines, as they have been called, do simple jobs such as paint spraying in car factories, and drilling holes in panels. That is to say, they carry out repetitive tasks. This early kind of machine would probably keep on spraying paint even if the car was not there, but the newer models are equipped with vision or sensors, enabling them to alter their behaviour according to their environment. They can sense what is going on around them: they could, for instance, navigate their way around a cluttered room.

These later developments will not necessarily replace the old ones: they will merely bring new applications in industry and commerce. One newly developed robot is a textile gripper. It can pick a single thin layer of cloth from the top of a high

(35 wpm)   pile. It does this by blowing air from the end of the robot arm, and when the top layer separates, the gripper - which looks

(40 wpm)   like the long thin beak of a pelican - is inserted, and it grabs the cloth ready for transfer to the work station. Another invention in the food industry has a colour inspection ability. It can tell whether cherry cakes have the prescribed number of

(50 wpm)   cherries, by recognising the amount of red in the cake. This process is much quicker than any human could manage.

Trials with the use of the human voice have been going on for a long time, and it now seems likely that robots will soon be

(60 wpm)   able to react to a human voice if it uses a small vocabulary and gives precise instructions. New uses for these devices are being thought up all the time, such as using them to handle high-speed water jets to clean out fuel tanks in an aircraft

(70 wpm)   factory. A job that would normally take two men a whole day to do in dangerous conditions can now be done mechanically in two or three hours.

Japan easily leads the robot business at present. America is

(80 wpm)   the next, and Britain comes sixth in a list of eleven countries.

RSAC II (Intermediate) Jan 1986

Minutes

Exercise 216 (Target time = 25 minutes)

Type the following Minutes of meeting, using side headings as shown.

Minutes of a Committee Meeting of the Windon Sports Club held at the Town Hall on 28 February 19-- at 7.30 pm.

Present

Mrs B Adams (Chairperson)   Miss P Johnson
Mr M Blackwood (Secretary)   Mr R Swindon
Mr R Daniels   Miss B Young

1	Apologies for absence	Apologies for absence were received from Miss A Jones and Mr K Worthing.
2	Minutes of the last meeting	The minutes of the last meeting, held on 20 December 19-- were read, approved and signed by the Chairperson.
3	Matters arising from the minutes	The complaint from the local authority regarding the excessive noise at the Fancy Dress Disco had been replied to by the Secretary. The Club had promised to take steps to prevent similar occurrences in the future.
		Metal grilles had now been fitted to the windows at the rear of the Club House to discourage vandalism and theft, as agreed at the last meeting. Members who had seen the grilles complimented the Secretary on the attractive design chosen, which fitted in with the design of the building as well as providing added security.
4	Correspondence	The Secretary read a letter from a local resident who complained the Club Members persistently parked across his driveway, preventing him from entering or leaving his drive by car. The Secretary agreed to write to Mr Gomal, the resident concerned, and Mr Daniels agreed to write a message to Members in the next Newsletter appealing for more thoughtfulness in parking.
5	Review of subscription rates	It was agreed that the subscription rates should be increased by 15% for Full Members and 10% for Old Age Pensioners and Junior Members, as from 1 May 19--.
6	Fund raising	Fund raising events during the past 6 months had raised £2,550. It was agreed that £2,000 of this should be allocated to the New Pavilion Fund, and the remainder to the Equipment Fund. Mr Daniels agreed to insert a short article in the Newsletter about the success of the Fund Raising Campaign.
7	Any other business	There was no other business.
8	Date of next meeting	It was agreed that the next meeting should be held in the Sterling Room at the Town Hall on 20 April 19--, at 7.30 pm.
9	Close of meeting	The Chairperson thanked the Committee Members for attending, and declared the meeting closed at 9.45 pm

Chairperson .... Date ....

Exercise 74

There is a very old and famous firm of watchmakers in Switzerland who turn out only twelve thousand watches a year, compared with some other well-known large firms who may make as many as ten times that number.

Each finished article takes at least nine weeks to produce. The craftsmen have to work all the time with powerful magnifying glasses that can indicate the thousandth part of a millimetre. The firm is capable of making a timepiece that can show the extra day in a Leap Year without any manual adjustment being needed. This is governed by a very slow mechanism that revolves once every four years. The raw materials that are used, such as gold, rubies and diamonds, are so valuable that the floors in the workshops have to be carefully swept very often, so that any tiny bits that have been dropped can be preserved. The doormats are taken up regularly and burned, so that gold can be retrieved from the ashes. In fact a large amount of gold is clawed back in this way.

The company aims to keep track of everything they sell. Each watch is therefore numbered, and entered in a ledger with the date of sale, and the name of the buyer. These items hardly ever disappear completely. Many of them are passed down within
(50 wpm) families to future generations, and if one that is particularly old and interesting does ever come up for sale, the firm's museum may well offer to buy it.

This firm and other Swiss makers are of course these days
(60 wpm) facing a strong challenge from the new quartz types from Japan, but the fact remains that the materials and jewels of the old watches are likely to last for ever.

In the meantime we ordinary people may go on buying quite cheap
(70 wpm) modern watches, not expecting them to last for long. Sometimes we may find that we can pick up a replacement, perhaps at the place where we buy our petrol, for even less money than it would cost us to buy a new battery for our existing watch.
(80 wpm) This is an item that we never had to bother about before.

RSA Stage III (Advanced), June 1986

Accuracy and speed development   **38**

Extract of minutes

Exercise 215 (Target time = 20 minutes)

Type the following extract from the Minutes of a meeting on A4 paper. Use shoulder headings as shown.

THE BRIDCORD DEVELOPMENT COMPANY LTD

MINUTES OF THE SECOND ANNUAL GENERAL MEETING

Held at Roma House, Buxton, on Monday 1 May 19-- at 1400 hrs.

```
Present - Mr A Mead, Chairman          Mr J Brown, Secretary
          Mr G Mead, Managing Director Mr A Pain, representing
          Mr D Cope)                   Messrs Pain & Co
          Mr D Day ) Directors         (Auditors)
          Mr A May )                   and thirty shareholders
```

1   APOLOGIES

    Apologies were received from Mrs R Williams.

2   MINUTES OF PREVIOUS MEETING

    The Minutes of the First Annual General Meeting held on 22 March 19--, were read and signed by the Chairman as being a correct record of the proceedings.

3   AUDITORS' REPORT

    Mr A Pain, of Messrs Pain & Co (the Company's Auditors), read their report upon the Company's Accounts and Balance Sheet.

4   REPORT AND ACCOUNTS

    With the consent of the meeting, the Directors' Report and Accounts were taken as read.

5   CHAIRMAN'S SPEECH

    The Chairman then addressed the meeting upon the Company's position and prospects, and replied to various questions raised by the shareholders. On the motion of the Chairman, seconded by Mr D Cope, it was RESOLVED that the Report and Accounts for the year ended 31 December 19--, as audited and certified by the Company's Auditors, and now submitted to the meeting, be and are hereby approved and adopted.

6   NEXT MEETING

    The date of the next Annual General Meeting was fixed for 3 May 19--.

The Chairman declared the meeting closed at 2050 hrs.

(Space for signature)

A Mead
CHAIRMAN

(Date of signing)

4 Underscoring, paper, centring headings

Underscoring

The correct way to underscore is to type the word first and then return the carriage to the beginning of the word, using the carriage release *not* the carriage return lever. Remember that the underscore is an upper-case character and that the shift key or shift lock must be used. Terminal punctuation, or punctuation at the end of a line, should not be underscored.

Exercise 75

Type the following.

a Men of age object <u>too much</u>, consult <u>too long</u>,

   adventure <u>too little</u>, repent <u>too soon</u>.

b The French phrase <u>joie de vivre</u> means 'joy of living'.

c It is a mistake to look too far ahead. Only one link in the chain

   of destiny can be handled at a time. - <u>Winston Churchill</u>.

d Figure work: 123.45   *e Ornamental borders:* <u>oxoxoxo</u> <u>-o-o-o-o-</u> <u>xxxxxxx</u>
              <u>678.90</u> 802.35

Exercise 76   Margin stops 15 – 75 pica, 20 – 80 elite

Type one perfect copy of the following. Leave one clear linespace below headings.

<u>TUNE IN - RADIO</u>

    A Gilbert and Sullivan evening from the Royal Albert Hall
will be planned to include excerpts from '<u>Patience</u>', '<u>Princess
Ida</u>' and '<u>The Yeoman of the Guard</u>'. Marcus Gray will conduct.

    A special recording will be made of Beethoven's '<u>Emperor</u>'
<u>Concerto</u> by the Russian-born pianist Vladimir Roskovitch.

<u>TUNE IN - TELEVISION</u>

    John Burbridge talks to Susan Lambert about her friend-
ship with L H Brian who based his third and last novel, '<u>The
Wild One</u>', on her life. The talk will be fully illustrated.

    In the first of a new series Maurice Gibson talks to Lady
Amelia Welby, widow of Sir Alfred Welby, who was imprisoned in
Japan and later banished without reason. Her latest book
'<u>Life Behind Bars</u>' will be discussed at some length.

    Future programmes will include talking to Bertram Riley.
He is a reporter based in Scotland, but is now working for
'<u>The Guardian</u>'.

Chairman's Agenda This may contain additional notes on each item and is therefore more detailed than the Agenda sent to other members. The right side is left free so that the Chairman can write in any decisions or other notes.

Exercise 214 (Target time = 20 minutes)

Type the following Chairman's Agenda. Leave the right-hand side of the page clear for the chairman's notes.

THE BRIDCORD DEVELOPMENT COMPANY LIMITED

AGENDA FOR THE SECOND ANNUAL GENERAL MEETING

To be held at Roma House, Buxton, on Monday 1 May 19-- at 1400 hours.

1 The Secretary to read the notice convening
   the meeting.   .
2 The Secretary to read the Minutes of the
   previous meeting.
3 The Auditors' Report to be read.
4 The Chairman to ask the meeting whether the
   Directors' Report and Accounts as printed
   and submitted shall be taken as read.
5 The Chairman to:
   (a) Address the meeting on the Company's
        position and prospects.
   (b) Move: 'That the Report and Accounts
        for the year ended 31 December 19--,
        as audited and certified by the
        Company's auditors, and now submitted
        to the meeting, be and are hereby
        approved and adopted'.
   (c) Call on Mr D Cope to second the motion.
   (d) Invite the shareholders to discuss any
        points arising out of the motion.
   (e) Reply to any questions.
   (f) Put the motion to the meeting and
        declare the result.
6 The Chairman to move: 'That the dividend
   recommended by the Directors, viz 15% on
   the Ordinary Shares for the year 19-- be
   and is hereby approved, and that the
   dividend be paid, less Income Tax, on
   15 May 19--, to those shareholders appearing on the Register of Members on 5 April
   19--'.
7 A shareholder to move: 'That Messrs Pain
   & Co, having agreed to continue in office
   as auditors for a further year, their fee
   be and is hereby fixed at £750'. Another
   shareholder to second the motion. The
   Chairman to put motion to meeting and
   declare result.
8 The Chairman to declare the proceedings
   at an end.

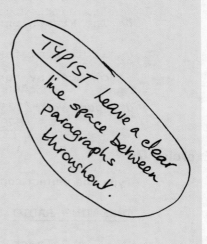

TYPIST leave a clear line space between paragraphs throughout.

Paper

The size of paper most widely used in offices is the international standard IPS (International Paper Sizes) which is based on metric measurement. The sizes of sheet most commonly used for letters, reports and similar documents are called A4 and A5 (there is also an intermediate size which has become known as two-thirds A4).

All sheets can be used either portrait, ie with the short side at the top, or landscape, with the long side at the top.

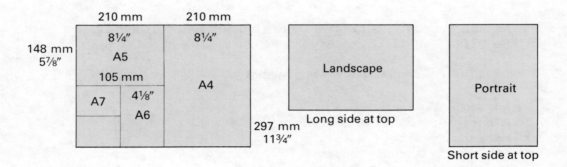

You must become familiar with the main paper sizes used in business and you should study the following table carefully. As sixmo, octavo and quarto sizes are still used in some places, they are included at the foot of the table.

Paper sizes and their uses

Name	Approximate dimensions		Uses
	Millimetres *length × width*	*Inches (approx)* *length × width*	
A7 (half A6)	78 × 105	2⅞ × 4⅛	Index cards, labels and dockets
A6 (half A5)	105 × 148	4⅛ × 5⅞	Index cards, postcards, memos, etc
A5 (half A4)	148 × 210	5⅞ × 8¼	Inter-departmental correspondence, short memos, personal correspondence and short business letters
'two-thirds' A4	200 × 210	5⅞ × 8¼	Business letters, memos, etc
A4	210 × 297	8¼ × 11¾	Long business and official letters, reports, etc
Foolscap (fcp.)	330 × 203	13 × 8	Long documents and legal work
Sixmo (6mo)	203 × 165	8 × 6½	Correspondence
Octavo (8vo)	203 × 127	8 × 5	Same uses as A5
Quarto (4to)	254 × 203	10 × 8	Same uses as A4

Spaces on a page
Read again page 6 Typewriter Type.

	Portrait			*Landscape*		
Spaces across paper	A4	A5	A6	A4	A5	A6
Pica	82	58	41	118	82	58
Elite	100	70	50	140	100	70
Lines down page	70	50	35	50	35	25

Watermarked paper

It will improve the appearance of your work and give it a 'professional touch' if you always type on the front or face of a sheet of paper. Hold the paper up to the light and look at the lettering or design in the watermark if any, and from this decide which is the face of the sheet.

Underscoring, paper, centring headings

Notice of Meeting, Agenda   These are frequently combined (see Exercise 212).

Exercise 212   (Target time = 8 minutes)

Type the following Notice of Annual General Meeting and Agenda.

THE WINDON GARDEN CLUB

24 January 19--

The Annual General Meeting of the Windon Garden Club will be held
in the Village Hall on Monday 21 February 19-- at 1930 hrs.

A G E N D A

1 Apologies.
2 Minutes of the last meeting.
3 Matters arising.
4 Chairman's Annual Report.
5 Secretary's Annual Report.
6 Treasurer's Annual Report and Accounts.
7 Election of:
   (a) Officers;
   (b) Committee.
8 To consider appointing and, if thought fit, to appoint a sub-
   committee of three members to arrange annual programme of
   social events.
9 Any other business.
10 Date and time of next meeting.

I WARD
Hon Secretary

Exercise 213   (Target time = 5 minutes)

Type the following agenda on A5 paper. Follow the layout indicated. This is an
extract from an RSA Examination paper.

A G E N D A
of Meeting 12 February 1986 @ 10.00 am

CHAIR ———→

1. Remitted items - meeting 2/1/86   V. C. Denning
2 Visit of executives from Sri Lanka   P. Langham
5 Presentation to L. J. Brierly   V. C. Denning
3 Monarch system   J. Frewin
4 Sales Report   E A Alderman

Align names with end of longest line, please

Displayed work

Centring headings

Subject headings are frequently used in letters or documents and may be centred in one of two styles:

1 Centred on the paper (when the margins are equal).
2 Centred on the writing line (when the margins are not equal).

Page width

To centre a heading, it is first necessary to know the total number of spaces across the page (see page 40).

1 Make sure the left edge of the paper is at 0 on the paper scale.
2 Using the paper scale, make a note of the number at the right edge of the paper.

Examples
In the examples on the next two pages A4 paper is used as an illustration (used portrait). There are 82 pica characters or 100 elite characters across an A4 sheet of paper. In the following text, those using elite machines should follow the figures in brackets.

Note There are two methods of centring (arithmetic and backspacing). You should study both methods then select the one which you find easier.

Arithmetic method

Style 1 (heading centred on the paper)
1 Find the total number of characters across the paper. On A4 this is 82 pica, 100 Elite.
2 Count the number of letters and spaces to be typed.
3 Subtract this from 82 (100).
4 Divide the remainder by 2 — this gives you the starting point for the heading.

For example, take the heading TYPEWRITING SPEEDS:

a There are 18 letters and spaces in the heading.
b Subtract 18 from 82 (100) and the remainder is 64 (82).
c Half of 64 is 32 and is the starting point for the heading on a pica machine.
Half of 82 is 41, which is the starting point for the heading on an elite machine.

Note If there is half a space over, eg, 31½, use the next number up, eg, 32.

**Starting
point
32 (41)**
↓
TYPEWRITING SPEEDS

Style 2 (heading centred on the writing line)
The calculations for this style are slightly different. Assume that you are going to use margin stops of 15 (25) and 75 (85) for the text of the letter or document:

1 Add the margin stop settings together, 15 + 75 = 90 (25 + 85 = 110).
2 Subtract 18 for the number of characters and spacing in the heading, 90 − 18 = 72 (110 − 18 = 92).

Documents for meetings

Layout

- Either the blocked or centred style may be used.
- At least one clear line space should be left between each part and above and below the headings.
- Capitals, spaced capitals and/or underscore may be used to highlight headings.
- Open or full punctuation may be used.

Notice of meeting

Exercise 210 (Target time = 4 minutes)

Type the following Notice of Meeting.

```
WINDON SPORTS CLUB

A meeting will be held in the Town Hall on Monday 28 February 19-- at
1930 hrs.  The Agenda will be circulated later.


R Daniels
Hon Secretary

88 Croften Road
SUNBURY

(Tel 09327 61387)
```

Agenda

Exercise 211 (Target time = 5 minutes)

Type the following Agenda. Leave one clear line space between agenda items.

```
THE WINDON SPORTS CLUB

Meeting to be held in the Victoria Room, Town Hall on Monday 28 February
19-- at 1930 hrs.

AGENDA

1  Apologies
2  Minutes of last meeting
3  Matters arising
4  Correspondence
5  Review of subscription rate
6  Fund-raising - achievements in past year
7  Any other business
8  Date of next meeting


R Daniels
Hon Secretary
```

3 Half of 72 is 36 and is the starting point for the heading on a pica machine.
  Half of 92 is 46 and is the starting point for the heading on an elite machine.

```
                              Starting
                              point
                              36 (46)
                              ↓
                              TYPEWRITING SPEEDS
15 (25)                                                              75 (85)
↓                                                                    ↓
xxxxxxxxxxxxxxxxxxxxxxxxxxxxxxxxxxxxxxxxxxxxxxxxxxxxxxxxxxxxxxxxxxxxxxxxxxxx
```

Backspace method

Style 1 (heading centred on the paper)

Another method of finding the correct starting point for a heading is to use the
backspacer. Take the same example as was used on the previous page — the
heading 'TYPEWRITING SPEEDS'.

1 It is first necessary to find the centre point of the sheet (divide the total by 2).
  If a sheet of A4 paper is in the machine with the left-hand edge at zero on the
  scale, the centre point is 41 for pica (50 for elite). Note that figures in brackets
  apply to elite machines.
2 Move the carriage to the centre point of the sheet and backspace once for
  every two letters and spaces in the heading.
3 Type the heading.

Note Ignore any characters left over.

```
                              Centre of sheet
                              41 (50)
                              ↓
                              TYPEWRITING SPEEDS
```

Style 2 (heading centred on the writing line)

Assume that you are going to use the same heading and that the margin stops for
the text of the letter or document are 15 (25) and 75 (85).

1 Add the margin stops together, $15 + 75 = 90$ $(25 + 85 = 110)$.
2 Divide by 2 (ignore fractions) and this will give you the centre point of your
  writing line — 45 (55). Move your carriage to this point and then backspace
  once for every 2 letters and spaces. Type the heading.

```
                              Centre of
                              line
                              45 (55)
                              ↓
                              TYPEWRITING SPEEDS
15 (25)                                                              75 (85)
↓                                                                    ↓
xxxxxxxxxxxxxxxxxxxxxxxxxxxxxxxxxxxxxxxxxxxxxxxxxxxxxxxxxxxxxxxxxxxxxxxxxxxx
```

Spaced capitals

Leave 1 space between each letter and 3 spaces between words.

```
T Y P E W R I T I N G   S P E E D S
```

Type the following notice. Follow the display directions given in the lower right-hand corner. This exercise formed part of a Higher Examination set by the London Chamber of Commerce and Industry.

RE-LOCATION OF OFFICE PREMISES
A CHECKLIST FOR THE ADMINISTRATOR

1. Office and Industrial Premises

    Are office and industrial premises built by the development corporation or by a private developer? Is land for your own development really going to be available? If so, when and on what conditions? A large number of new towns are currently developing office premises (which have tended to lag behind shop and ~~other~~ building) for occupation the by end of 1988. Other development corporations still tend to be somewhat 'light' on office availability or plants.

    [margin left: Industrial] *[margin right: trs]*

2. Employment

    Is the professional office, skilled or general plant labour you need likely to be available, or will you have (absurdly) to 'commute' them from the big city or bring some or all of them with you?

(caps) 3. Transport and Communications
    Check for nearby motorway access, railway stations (some new towns still have not got one), ports & container concentration points, airports.

(caps) 4. Rents and prices, In the run-up period try constantly to monitor shop, office factory and warehouse rents or freehold prices and land prices in the new towns you are considering. Do not assume that remoteness from a major conurbation will necessarily hold rents down.

6. Homes
    Is housing adequately available? Are there preferential rental or purchase schemes for newly-arrived employees? Is there suitable accommodation for the elderly dependents some of the families of your staff may wish to bring with them?

5. Office Development Permits, Is your chosen new town effectively reserved for the re-location of existing local industry and commerce? Are ODPs required or hard to get? If either, look elsewhere unless you are determined to press your case and your business is small enough to stand a chance.

(in full)

TYPIST: Please display the list of points in two columns, like this:

```
1. __    4. __
2. __    5. __
3. __    6. __
```

The paras. should be numbered.

Exercise 77

1 Centre the heading 'TYPEWRITING SPEEDS' on an A4 sheet of paper, first using unspaced capitals, then using spaced capitals.
2 Centre the heading over the writing line given, first using unspaced capitals, then using spaced capitals.

Exercise 78

Centre the following three headings on an A4 sheet of paper.

THE BRITISH ISLES
THE ART OF PUBLIC SPEAKING
A STUDY OF AFRICA

Exercise 79

Centre the heading in Exercise 77 on the writing line, using margin stops 20 – 70 pica, 30 – 80 elite.

Exercise 208 (Target time = 25 minutes)

Type a copy of the following Estate Agent's property details. Follow the layout and capitalisation shown.

NIGEL CROSBY & PARTNERS
(E and A Crosby)
Auctioneers and Estate Agents

---

178 Western Road   Brookbridge   Suffolk   Brookbridge 67418

43 Lavington Road, BROOKBRIDGE

An attractive DETACHED HOUSE with colour-rendered elevations under a pantiled roof. In excellent decorative order and with spacious accommodation.

Situated in this much sought after area close to excellent shopping facilities and within easy distance of Golf Course, the Town Centre and Railway Station.

The accommodation, with approximate room measurements, comprises:

ENTRANCE PORCH   leading to ENTRANCE HALL with fitted cupboard, telephone and
                 hot-water radiator.

LOUNGE   15' 0" x 12' 10". Attractive tiled fireplace, tiled hearth.
                 Night storage heater. Power points. Glazed doors leading to

DINING ROOM   12' 4" x 12' 0". Attractive tiled fireplace and hearth. Glazed
                 door to garden. Wall lights. Power points.

KITCHEN   15' 0" x 12' 0". Single-drainer enamelled sink unit (h & c)
                 with drawer and cupboard under. Tiled walls. Electric water
                 heater. Range of floor units providing worktop and storage
                 space. Walk-in larder. Large storage cupboard. Airing cup-
                 board with hot-water tank. Ideal domestic boiler. Power points.

FIRST FLOOR

LANDING   Night storage heater. Access to roof space.

BEDROOM 1   15' 0" x 12' 0". Tiled fireplace. Built-in cupboard. Power
                 points. Hot-water radiator.

BEDROOM 2   12' 4" x 12' 0". Tiled fireplace. Built-in cupboard. Power
                 point.

BEDROOM 3   10' 6" x 7' 0". Power point.

BATHROOM   Modern panelled bath (h & c). Pedestal washhand basin
                 (h & c). Half-tiled walls. Electric wall-heater.

SEPARATE WC   Low-level suite.

OUTSIDE

GARAGE   15' 0" x 8' 6". Water tap. Power and light.   SEPARATE WC
FUEL STORE   and paved area with GARDEN SHED.

GARDENS   Easily managed rear garden laid to lawn and flower borders.
                 Attractive front and side gardens with lawn and flowering shrubs.

ASSESSMENTS   Rateable Value £258. General and Water Rates £758.66 pa

VIEWING BY APPOINTMENT   PRICE £105,000 FREEHOLD

These particulars are believed to be correct but the accuracy is in no way guaranteed nor do they form part of a contract.

Displayed work   **124**

5 The correction of errors, typing from manuscript

The correction of errors

If you know you have made an error, correct it before going on. Read through the whole page before removing it from the machine. Careful proofreading will make corrections much easier to carry out.

If you do not discover an error until after the work has been taken out of the machine, the erasure can be made, the sheet replaced, and the correction typed in with the help of the alignment scale.

Methods of correction

Rubber Turn up the paper so that the error is on the cylinder or paper table. If possible move the carriage to the extreme left or right, so that the dust will not fall inside the machine. Hold the paper firmly and erase gently. After you have made the erasure, you should blow the dust away from the machine. Then return the line to the printing position.

Correction paper Backspace to the letter or word to be erased, place the strip of correction paper over the error with the printed side towards you and retype the same error through the strip. Remove the correction paper and type in the correct letter.

Correction fluid This fluid can be obtained to match the shade of paper you are using. Using a brush you merely paint over the error, allow the fluid to dry, and retype over the top.

Correction ribbons Most electric/electronic typewriters have a correction ribbon fitted. The exact method of operation will vary from one machine to another, but the correction ribbon makes correcting errors relatively easy. Check your machine manual for instructions.

Half-space correcting Occasionally you may have to make a correction that involves erasing a word containing, say, three characters, and typing in its place one containing four. When the backspacer is pressed down only half-way the printing point moves to the left only half a space.

For example if you have to substitute the word 'many' for the word 'few', the word 'few' should first be erased, and the carriage moved so that the printing point is at the space formerly occupied by the 'f'. Using the backspacer, move half a space to the left and type the 'm' of 'many', repeat for the 'a' of 'many', then the 'n' and 'y'.

When the space bar is pressed down and held the carriage has moved half a space to the right. Releasing the bar allows the carriage to move the other half-space. For example, suppose you have to insert the word 'few' in place of 'many'. First, erase the wrong word and then return to the printing point previously occupied by the 'm'. Now, hold down the space bar and type 'f' and release the bar. Repeat this whole operation for the 'e' and the 'w' and you will find that the word 'few' has one and a half spaces before and after it.

When either of these methods of half-space correcting is used, the space before and after the new word is, of course, different from the standard. Electric and electronic typewriters generally have a half-space correction key. Check your machine manual for instructions.

Itinerary

An 'itinerary' is a personal programme or list of important events and times concerning a visit to be made by an individual or a group of people. Visits by your employer which will involve rail or air travel, hotel reservations, etc., should always show clearly the train-departure station and times, arrival time at destination, airline, flight numbers, airports, check-in and departure times, arrival times in home and local times, name and address of hotel, telegraphic/telex and telephone numbers, etc. Copies of the itinerary should be sent to all those who may be concerned with the arrangements. For example, if the Transport Manager is not told, it could well happen that the company car will not be waiting for the Managing Director at 0930 hrs (Exercise 206). The following exercise is a simple itinerary for a visit by the Managing Director of a caravan company (Mr C K Robinson) to his company's stand at a Caravan Exhibition.

Exercise 206 (Target time = 12 minutes)

Type a copy of the following itinerary, on A5 paper.

C A R A V A N   E X H I B I T I O N

ITINERARY

Mr C K Robinson's visit on 28 October 19--

0930 hrs   Depart Head Office by car.

1100 hrs   Arrive at Exhibition Hall to meet Marketing
Director (Mr J Woods) at main entrance.
Inspection of stand and talks with:
Home Sales Manager and Representatives;
Overseas Sales Managers; and Production
Manager.

1200 hrs   Short tour of remainder of exhibition,
accompanied by Marketing Director and
Production Director.

1300 hrs   Lunch with Marketing Director and Production
Director.

1430 hrs   Return to Exhibition Hall to meet the
company's main home and overseas agents and
customers.

1600 hrs   Depart exhibition.

Distribution: Company Secretary's Office (2)
Transport Manager (2)
Marketing Department (10)
Production Department (4)

Exercise 207 (Target time = 12 minutes)

Retype the above exercise using blocked style for the headings. Use open punctuation style.

Feeding paper backwards into the typewriter   If you have to make a correction on one of several sheets which are fastened together at the top without removing the fastener, this can be done by 'backward feeding'. First insert a loose sheet of paper into the machine in the ordinary way. Then feed in the bottom of the page to be corrected *from the front,* between the loose sheet and the platen. When this page is in position, remove the loose sheet by using the paper-release lever. Take care, of course, to adjust the page to the exact position before typing the correction.

Proofreading

Proofreading (checking for errors) is a vital part of the typing task. All work produced must be mailable (without error) otherwise it is of no use at all.

● Always check your work before removing it from the machine, otherwise correction of errors is more difficult.
● Read word for word (some errors are not obvious at a glance) and check all figures with the original.

Type of error	Example	Correct copy
Spelling	the feild	the field
Punctuation, grammar	Order one, two three or	Order one, two, three or
Substitution errors	pay the pay you fare	pay them pay your fare
Typographical (wrong key struck)	pat your fare	pay your fare
Wrong, or inconsistent spacing	paythe be fore today .	pay the before today.
Figures incorrect	£61.09	£61.90
Inconsistent use of capitals	the Bank holiday	The Bank Holiday
Words commonly confused	effect/affect lose/loose	

Typing from manuscript

Typing from straightforward manuscript

A manuscript is any document written by hand. Always read through the whole of a manuscript to become acquainted with its subject and with the handwriting before beginning to type. This will often help you with the recognition of unusual and sometimes not very legible words.

Reports

The style of a report may be indicated by the author. If no guidelines are given, the following paragraphs will prove a useful general guide:
When using decimal enumerations leave 2 clear spaces after the numbers.

Exercise 205 (Target time = 25 minutes)

Read and type the following report, which itself contains information on the typing of reports.

1   PAPER

Use good quality paper, A4 size. Type on one side only unless instructed otherwise.

2   SPACING, MARGINS AND PAGINATION

This will depend upon the length of the report and the purpose for which it is being typed.

2.1 Spacing. Use single spacing unless instructed otherwise.

2.2 Margins. The left margin should not be less than 1" (25 mm) and the right not less than ½" (13 mm). However, if the report is to be bound on the left side, leave 1½" (38 mm).

2.2.1   Top and bottom margins should be equal - usually 1" (25 mm).

2.2.2   Put a light pencil mark at the bottom of the sheet or use a backing sheet with a heavy line to show the bottom margin. You may also do this for the top to save time and ensure consistency. Remember to erase the pencil mark when you have completed your work.

2.3 Pagination. Do not number the first page. Other pages may be numbered at the top or bottom, at the left or right margin or centred (consistently).

3   HEADINGS

Headings and sub-headings often make a report easier to understand. It is essential that they are used consistently throughout the document and that spacing is consistent.

4   CATCHWORDS

When a continuation sheet is used a 'catchword' may be typed at the foot of the page. The first word (or two) of the next page is typed below the last line ending at the right margin. Alternatively, 'PTO' or 'Continued' may be used.

Typing from manuscript containing abbreviations or corrections

When people are writing out material which is to be typed, they often use simple but time-saving abbreviations. As they are writing they are also likely to make changes to the wording, deleting some words, inserting others and providing instructions about the display of the document.

The typist is expected to type abbreviated words in full, wherever this is appropriate. Some words will, of course, be left in their abbreviated form, such as et al, ie, viz, eg, Mr or Mrs. Others will be typed in full in continuous text, but may sometimes be left abbreviated, eg, the 'ampersand' & or *&* should always be typed in full in a sentence, but may be retained as an abbreviation in the name of a firm as in 'Kanu & Olega Limited'.

Instructions for correcting and altering the draft should always be carried out accurately and with care.

Abbreviations used in drafting documents

You should know the following abbreviations and always type them in full.

accommodation	*accom*	from	*fr.*	shall	*sh*
account	*a/c*	full-time	*ft*	should	*shd*
acknowledge	*ack.*	government	*gov.*	signature	*sig.*
advertisement	*advert.*	guarantee	*gntee*	sufficient	*suff.*
although	*altho'*	hours	*hrs*	temporary	*temp.*
and	*&*	immediately	*immed*	that	*th*
appointment	*appt.*	information	*info*	through	*thro'*
approximately	*approx.*	manufacturer	*mfr*	which	*wh*
as soon as possible	*asap.*	miscellaneous	*misc.*	would	*wd*
believe	*bel.*	necessary	*necy.*	with	*w*
business	*bus.*	opportunity	*opp.*	will	*wl*
catalogue	*cat.*	organisation	*org.*	year	*yr*
committee	*cttee*	part-time	*p/t*	your	*yr*
company	*co.*	possible	*poss*		
companies	*cos.*	receipt	*rec.*	days of the week	
could	*cd*	receive	*rec.*	(eg Thurs, Fri)	
dear	*dr*	received	*recd.*	months of the year	
definitely	*def.*	recommend	*recom.*	(eg Jan, Feb)	
develop	*dev.*	refer	*ref.*	words in addresses	
especially	*esp.*	referred	*refd.*	(eg St, Cres)	
exercise	*ex.*	responsible	*resp.*	complimentary close	
expense	*exp.*	secretary	*sec.*	(eg ffly)	
experience	*exp.*	separate	*sep.*		

The writer may or may not include a full stop after the abbreviation.

The following exercises will give you practice in typing from simple, straightforward manuscript and each has a heading. Begin typing approximately 1" from the top of the sheet (turn up 7 or 8 spaces).

Type the following Notice of Auction. Follow the layout shown.

FOR SALE BY AUCTION

BY DIRECTION OF THE THOMAS ROBINSON TRUST

I N   T H E   H E A R T

of the

S O U T H   D O W N S

Between Chichester and Midhurst, 2 miles from Singleton
10 miles from Petersfield, and 6 miles from Chichester

The Residential, Sporting and Agricultural Estate known as

B R O W N L O W   P A R K

2,004 ACRES

SUMMARY

Lot	Holding						Acres
1	Warnford Lodge	...	...	...	...	...	507.86
2	High Cross Farm	...	...	...	...	...	473.24
3	West Hinton Farm	...	...	...	...	...	450.40
4	Brownlow House and Garden		...	...	...	32.75
5	Riverside Grazing	...	...	...	...	...	38.66
6	Well Farm	...	...	...	...	...	...	410.44
7	South Woods	...	...	...	...	...	...	12.80
8	Large Paddock	...	...	...	...	...	17.25
9	Small Paddock	...	...	...	...	...	1.50
10	Weston Pasture	...	...	...	...	...	12.10
11	Brook Nursery	...	...	...	...	...	7.40
12	Grayshott Farm	...	...	...	...	...	40.10
						Total	2,004.50

JOHNSON and BLAKE will offer the Estate as a whole, or in
lots, at the Bell Hotel, Chichester, on Wednesday,
14 August, 19--, at 1400 hrs precisely (unless previously
sold by Private Treaty).

Exercise 80

Type in the indented style, using double-line spacing. Use A4 paper (portrait) and centre the heading on the page. Type the heading in capitals. Leave one clear space below the heading (turn up two spaces).

Applying for a Job

There is an art in reading advertisements which give details of offers of employment. If you study them carefully, you will find they give a good deal of information which is far beyond the bare facts of the vacant post. For instance, the style and general appearance of the advertisement almost always reflect the nature of the company. A dull and rather staid layout suggests a firm which matches its advertisement. The choice of words is very important, too.

Exercise 81

Now retype the same piece using blocked paragraph style. Note that when you are using blocked paragraph style you may block the heading at the left margin *or* centre it. Use A4 paper (portrait) and single-line spacing. Leave 1 clear line space below the heading (turn up 2 spaces).

Exercise 82

Type in the indented style (single-line spacing). Use A5 paper (landscape) and centre the heading on the writing line. Heading to be typed in capitals.

Seat Belts in Motor Vehicles

Everyone in the motor industry, in the medical profession and in government departments concerned with transport believes that seat belts save lives. Recent figures suggest that some thirty thousand deaths and serious injuries would be avoided annually in the United Kingdom, for example, if everyone used the protection which is available to them. It is calculated that at present less than half of the motorists in England use their belts on motorways, but the figure falls below twelve per cent in towns

Exercise 83

Type Exercise 82 in the blocked style (single-line spacing). Use A5 paper (landscape). You may type the heading at the left margin or centred over the typing line.

Exercise 202 (Target time = 10 minutes)

Display the following programme effectively in whichever style you prefer.

LACEY HILL GARDEN SOCIETY , JULY PROGRAMME . Tues 2/7/-- Coffee Morning 10·30am , including a Bring & Buy Stall . Thurs 12 July 7·30 pm Film with Sound Track entitled 'The Rose'. Competition for the evening — Vase of cut Flowers or Sprays of Flowering Shrubs . Sat 21 July . Outing to Rayford Park, Rayford . Full details later . Will members please note dates in their diaries . Lawn Spreader — Members are reminded that a Lawn Spreder is available for their use & may be borrowed from the Hon. Sec. Mr. J. F. Newman , 26 Dobey Avenue , Rother Vale. Telephone R.V. 2601 (evenings only)

[margin note: :ROTHER: 12" a]

Exercise 203 (Target time = 20 minutes)

Type the following programme on A4 paper. Inset programme items 5 spaces from left margin as indicated. Justify the times at the right margin and use leader dots in place of the dashes.

(spaced caps) — PROGRAMME FOR THE DAY (Typist — 1 +1 carbon please)

Sports Arena

Motor Racing — the French Grand Prix — 1455
Swimming — Sweden v Gt. Britain — 1530
Horse Jumping — All Eng. Finals — 1600
Wrestling : Bob Cross v L. Paget — 1630
" Dave Barker v Johnny Mathews —1700

Religion

Morning Service — 10·30
Religious Discussions — 18 15
Sunday Story (for Children) — 18 45
Choral Evensong (from Bradford Cathedral)— 1830
Songs of Praise — 1900 (from St Cuthbert's Church Ipswich)

Farming & Gardening (Question & Answer Time)

Gardening Club — 13 15
Farmers' Report (Weekly) — 1330
Weather — 1345

(2100 News -1800 & Weather -2130)

The Theatre

Treasure Island — 1315
Much Ado about Nothing — 1450

(Serial in 20 parts)

Music

Your Concert Choice (Request Programme) — 1550
Mozart & Beethoven – A Musical Magazine — 1630

Films

Gandhi — 1420
Out of Africa — 2000

Book Reviews

Cry, the Beloved Country } 2200
The Moon's a Balloon

Exercise 84

Type in the indented style using single-line spacing. Use A5 paper landscape and centre the heading on the page in capitals. Leave 1 clear space between the paragraphs (turn up 2 spaces). Decide on your own margins.

Invoices

In modern business, invoices are usually printed in two or more copies, with serial numbers. The firm's name and address, etc. are printed on the form; and space is left for the name and address of the buyer of the goods. The rest of the form is ruled in columns so that the quantities, prices and value of each purchase, together with the total amount can be clearly seen.

Invoices will state when payment is expected, and what cash discount will be allowed for prompt payment.

Exercise 85

Now retype the same piece in the blocked style, using single-line spacing. Use A5 paper portrait. You may block or centre the heading.

Exercise 86

Type Exercise 84 in the blocked style (double-line spacing). Remember that when typing in single-line spacing, you should turn up two spaces between paragraphs. In double-line spacing there should always be more space between paragraphs than there is between lines — it is easiest to turn up twice (leaving 3 clear spaces).

Exercise 87

Type in the indented style (double-line spacing). Centre the heading on the page in capitals. Use suitable paper.

Fish Farming

The fishermen of the world are becoming so efficient that they are well on the way to causing a serious reduction in the world's stock of fish. There is therefore widespread interest in efforts to develop fish farming, that is to rear fish in much the same way as a farmer grows corn. Cultivating fish in fresh water has, of course, been practised for centuries but the possibility, as well as the difficulty, of rearing fish in salt water has been considered only comparatively recently. Japan and Great Britain are the leaders in this field.

Exercise 200 (Target time = 5 minutes)

Type the following display. Use leader dots in groups of 2. Justify items at the right margin.

<pre>
            SPECIAL WINTER CLOTHING OFFER

Man's full length woollen coat £189.95
Lady's short suede coat £175.50
Boy's leather jacket £85.50
Girl's fun-fur midi-coat £75.75
</pre>

Exercise 201 (Target time = 10 minutes)

Type the following programme. Follow the display shown. Insert leader dots.

<pre>
              PARISH CHURCH OF ST AUGUSTINE
                        OXBRIDGE

                   'HERE WE MAKE MUSIC'
          presented by a section of the Choir of
                 Letchbury Parish Church

               directed by NIGEL WINDSOR

               with RAYMOND MILLER Oboe

               and ANTHONY LOWE Continuo

            Poetry Readings by NANCY STEELE

ANTHEMS

If ye love me, keep my commandments .. .. THOMAS TALLIS (1505-1585)
Sing we merrily   .. .. ADRIAN BATTEN (1585-1637)

ORGAN (Nigel Windsor)

Two pieces for a Musical Clock   .. .. JOSEPH HAYDN (1732-1809)

POETRY

To be announced

OBOE AND CONTINUO

Arioso   .. .. J H FIOCCO (1703-1741)
Where'er you Walk .. .. G F HANDEL (1685-1759)

                    I N T E R V A L
</pre>

Correction signs

The signs given in the table below are conventional ones used on handwritten or typewritten work as indications to a typist that changes are required when the final copy is being typed.

Change required	*Indication in text*
Change to capital letters	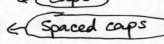
Change to space capital letters	← Spaced caps
Change to lower case (small letters)	The capital letter(s) is/are struck through or underlined thus: When or WHEN; or When or WHEN
Transpose (change the order or position(s) of)	Change order horizontally ⌣ Change order vertically
Insert a full stop or other punctuation mark (at the point indicated by the 'caret' ⋏)	
Omit and replace	Clearly crossed through — replacement material written above if possible or in balloon with caret sign
Additional material	Written in balloon. Caret sign shows position.
Insert space (where indicated by the caret sign).	#
Begin a fresh paragraph at the point indicated	[or //
No fresh paragraph	marked at point where the change is required
Omit the letter(s) or word(s) struck through	It is is unnecessary
Let the original word(s) stand	A dotted line under the matter wrongly struck through or changed eg *car* Ø may be shown in margin.
No space required between the words or characters marked	'To day' is one word
Word not clear in text	MEXICO made clearer in margin with broken line around word

Note Always check foreign or unfamiliar words by using a dictionary or referring to the author.

Leader dots

If there is a risk that the reader's eye will not easily link words or figures on the left with related words or figures on the right, a series of full stops known as leader dots is used as the 'link'. The following are examples of 3 different styles of leader dots:

```
Displays ..    ..    ..    ..    ..    ..    ..    ..    .. 1,298
Showcases      ..    ..    ..    ..    ..    ..    ..    ..   145

Window Lettering ...  ...  ...  ...  ...  ...  ...  ... 9,747
Showcards    ...  ...  ...  ...  ...  ...  ...  ...  ... 4,686

Dummy Boxes ....................................... 6,350
Stands ............................................. 1,994
```

- Leader dots may be typed as a continuous line of dots, or in groups of two or three dots at regular intervals.
- Always leave at least one space between the word and the start of the leader dots.
- Always leave at least one space between the last leader dot and the following figures or words.
- Where groups of 2 or 3 dots are used, ensure that the groups of dots are aligned evenly.
- Do not start or finish a line with only part of a group.
- Continuous dots are quickest and easiest to type, but whichever style you select, it should be used consistently throughout a document.
- Use your own judgement to decide when leader dots are needed.

Justified right margin

For displays with a justified right margin, use equal margins. Set a tab stop at the right-hand margin point. When you are ready to type a justified item, move to the tab stop position and backspace once for *each* character in the word or number, then type the item.

Exercise 198   (Target time = 8 minutes)

Type the examples shown above on A5 paper. Centre the heading TYPES OF LEADER DOTS over the display.

Exercise 199   (Target time = 5 minutes)

Type the following display on A5 paper. Use continuous leader dots and justify the right margin.

```
            COMPUTER PRINTERS - SALE PRICE

Brinscoe M2799 ............................. £435.75
Brinscoe Twin-Writer ....................... £660.15
Hammond Laser-Writer ....................... £999.99
Fallora A220 ............................... £535.50
```

Exercise 88

Type the following, choosing your own style of display and size of paper.

TRADE DISCOUNTS

Trade discounts vary enormously depending on the trade or industry concerned. They are normally referred to as a percentage of the manufacturer's recommended selling price, viz. the retail price paid by the public. It is obvious that the manufacturer must make a reduction to the retailer in order to encourage him to sell the goods. In the most simple cases trade discount is, in effect, the gross profit of the retailer. Trade discount can be regarded as a normal means of reducing the advertised or catalogue price to the real selling price of the supplier to the retailer.

Exercise 89

Type the following, choosing your own style of display and size of paper.

THE IMPORTANCE OF NEWSPAPERS

Newspapers play a very important part in our lives. It is true, of course, that over fifty years ago, when there was little or no domestic radio and no television, newspapers were much more important to people than they are today.

It is interesting to observe, however, that although the newspapers were in those days the only source of news, the circulation of the papers was much less than it is today, when information on a great variety of events all over the world can be heard on the radio and seen on television.

Almost everybody buys some kind of newspaper, and some people buy two or three each day.

Exercise 192 (Target time = 7 minutes)

Type a copy of the formal invitation shown below on A5 paper. Follow the layout shown.

Mr and Mrs John Smith	Mr and Mrs A Townsend
request the pleasure of the company of	have much pleasure
. . . .	in accepting the invitation of
at the marriage of their daughter	Mr and Mrs J Smith
Anne Elizabeth	to the wedding
to Mr David Eric Taylor	of their daughter
at St Paul's Church, Eastwood, Sussex	on Saturday 18 March 19--
on Saturday 18 March 19--	
at 12 noon	
and afterwards at the Ivy Bridge Hotel	

14 Linden Avenue   RSVP   26 Cedar Avenue
Eastwood   Newport
Sussex   Gwent
EW6 3LJ   NP1 5RF   1 March 19--

Exercise 193 (Target time = 5 minutes)

Type a copy of the formal acceptance shown above on A5 paper. Follow the layout shown.

Exercise 194 (Target time = 8 minutes)

Type and display the following formal invitation using the blocked style.

The Chairman and Directors of Worldwide Construction Ltd. request the pleasure of the company of . . . . at lunch at the Spa Hotel, Humberside, at 1 p.m. on Thursday, 10 May 19-- to precede the official opening of the new Sports Centre by the Rt. Hon. the Lord Mayor of Humberside. The Secretary, Worldwide Construction Ltd., London. R.S.V.P.

Exercise 195 (Target time = 6 minutes)

Type and display a formal acceptance of the invitation in Exercise 194 on behalf of yourself using the blocked style.

Exercise 196 (Target time = 7 minutes)

Type and display the following formal invitation.

Captain & Mrs. H.R. Manning request the pleasure of the co. of - - - - - - - at a Dinner to celebrate their Golden Wedding at the Waldorf Hotel, Southampton on Saturday, 14 April 19-- at ~~7pm~~. 7.30pm. Fenchurch House, Blueberry Hill, Southampton SO4 2XY RSVP

Exercise 197 (Target time = 6 minutes)

Type and display a formal acknowledgement of the invitation for yourself in Exercise 196, apologising for your inability to attend because of absence abroad.

Exercise 90

Type in the indented style (double-line spacing). There are 6 spelling errors that should be corrected. Type ordinal numbers (1st, etc) in full. Proofread and correct your work before removing it from the machine.

WOMEN AT WORK

Nowadays it is the most natural thing for women to go out into the world to earn their own living. The salary or wages paid for the work done varies considerably. Some women earn quiet a small amount of money, while others can earn ~~bigger~~ large sums. Women ✓ holding top positions in bus. are often as highly paid as there male colleagues.

The income of a working woman depends upon several factors. 1st, the amt. of time she is able to devote to her ocupation. 2nd, the kind of education she has had. 3rd, the particular carear th she has chosen and finely, how easily she can be replaced.

Exercise 91

Type Exercise 90 again but in the blocked style (single-line spacing).

Exercise 92

Type the following. Correct 4 spelling errors.

Credit Cards → Centre in caps

Credit cards, if carefully used, can provide short-term, interest-free credit because about 25 days are allowed for settlement of a monthly bill before any interest is due. So by planned, careful spending + by paying particular attention to the calender regarding payments, it is poss. for people to have all the conveniance of shopping without cash + the use of a bank's credit facilities without charge. If however, a debt is carried over to a 2nd yr., things become expensive because interest is payable on the outstanding 1st year's interest, + this can make the originel perchase more expensive than intended!

Exercise 189 (Target time = 12 minutes)

Type the following menu on A4 paper. Follow the layout shown. Type the horizontal line from margin to margin. If there are no accent keys on your typewriter, write in the accents on your completed menu with matching ink.

THE BELMONT HOTEL AT LITTLETON

M E N U

DINNER £15.50 (inc VAT)   SATURDAY 9 AUGUST 19--

Pâté Maison   Cream of Chicken
Iced Fruit Juices   Melon Frappé
                    Consommé en Tasse

                         -o-o-o-

                Grilled Halibut Steak Sauce Tartare
                Roast Breast of Chicken à l'Anglaise
                      Lamb Cutlets Reformé
                 Calves' Sweetbreads à la Crème
                  Grilled Rump Steak Vert Pré

Buttered Runner Beans   Boiled Potatoes
Cauliflower Mornay   Roast Potatoes

                         -o-o-o-

Fresh Fruit Salad and Cream   Gâteau Maison
Peach Melba   Meringue Glacée
                  Cheese and Biscuits

                         -o-o-o-

                        Coffee 65p

Exercise 190 (Target time = 10 minutes)

Type the following advertisement. Display attractively on suitable paper. Use capitals, spaced capitals and underscoring to enhance the display.

Classical concert, Town Hall, Bristol, Saturday 9 August 19-- at 8 pm. Admission £7.50. Tickets available from booking office, Main Street, from 9.30 am Tuesday 5 August. Book early to avoid disappointment.

Exercise 191 (Target time = 10 minutes)

Display the following advertisement attractively on suitable paper. Use capitals, spaced capitals and underscoring to enhance the display.

EMPIRE STORES — Sales Staff — We require several people aged between 18 and 30 to work in our Sporting Goods Department — Hours 9 am to 5 pm — Starting salary depends on age and experience — For further information apply to the Store Manager at 114 Main Street, Birmingham

Exercise 93

Type the following, correcting 3 spelling errors.

(centre) ⟵ ⟶ WINDOW BOXES

A window box can be far more than a container for growing plants—be it made of metal, (stone, wood) or plastic. It shd be decorative & fit in with its surroundings, but as the main decoration is obtained from the flowers or plants themselves, nothing shd be done to detract fr there beauty. Window boxes can be used very affectively for spring-flowering bulbs &, of course, for summer-flowering plants to give an almost continuous display.⟶

(extensive)

⟋This kind of plant container, including the ˅variety of tubs now produced by the plastics industry, can be used to cover vital but unsightly objects, & can do much to improve the appearance of patios, ✓ (terraces,) & large paved areas.

Exercise 94

Type the following, correcting 1 spelling error.

(caps) → German laws ⟶ centre (Some of)

⟋The household laws in Germany are very difficult to beleive. For example, net curtains must be hung on any windows wh overlook a main road & all shutters must be closed by sunset. Cars must not be cleaned on public holidays or Sundays & no washing may be hung out on these ~~two~~ days. Children are not allowed to play on the streets & all (television & radio) sets must be turned down very low at 2000 hrs. If snow falls, then the part of the road in front of your house must be cleared within 24 hours of the fall. If someone slips on, say, a leaf outside your front door, you cd be sued. ⎡If these laws are not observed, the police ~~will~~ may # very soon be calling!

Exercise 186 (Target time = 8 minutes)

Type the following menu on A5 paper in blocked style.

```
M E N U

BELVEDERE HOTEL


Lunch: £17.50 (inc VAT)

*******

Chilled Juices (Tomato, Orange and Pineapple)
Cream of Vegetable Soup

*******
Fried Fillet of Haddock
Braised Liver and Onions
Hot Roast Beef with Horseradish Sauce
Cold Ham and Salad
Fresh Scotch Salmon and Salad

Roast and Creamed Potatoes
Buttered Carrots
Mixed Vegetables

*******
Steamed Chocolate Sponge and Custard
Semolina with Pineapple
Peach Melba
Strawberry Ice Cream

*******
Coffee
```

Exercise 187 (Target time = 10 minutes)

Type the following menu on A5 paper in blocked style.

The Shamrock Hotel Lunch £10.60 Chilled Fruit Juices Scotch Broth Grilled Plaice with Tartar Sauce Scotch Salmon Salad Braised Steak and Onions Roast Leg of Lamb and Mint Sauce Cold Ham Ox Tongue with Salad Buttered Cabbage Roast and Boiled Potatoes Baked Apple Compote of Rhubarb and Custard Ice Cream and Fruit Salad Coffee

Exercise 188 (Target time = 10 minutes)

Display the following menu in blocked style on A5 paper.

Business Lunch £9.75   THE CHELSEA ARMS HOTEL
Honeydew Melon Prawn Cocktail Egg Mayonnaise Grilled Trout
Fried Scampi Lamb Cutlets Pork Chop & Apple Sauce Sirloin
Steak (75p extra) Lamb's Liver & Bacon French Fried Pots Garden
Peas Runner Beans Cream Caramel Apple Pie & Fresh Cream Peach Melba
Ice Cream Cheese & Biscuits Coffee Aylesbury Duckling Gammon
Steak & Pineapple Fresh Salmon Salad Sprouts

Exercise 95

Type the following, correcting 2 spelling errors.

International Golf. [Spaced caps]

[now] There are far more oportunities than ever for playing golf in almost every country in the world - esp. in the popular holiday areas. [¶] Many British holiday brochures include a whole range of golfing holidays in Spain, Portugal, Italy, Switzerland, Greece, France & Tunisia (& these even extend to such places as the islands of Tenerife & Corfu). # [¶] The chosen centres often offer additional attractions of scenery, entertainment & sightseeing. [Just] golfing holiday resorts offer straight golf or golf with other interesting pastimes. [in other words, these.]

Exercise 96

Type the following. Choose your own layout style. Arrange the items in alphabetical order and correct where necessary.

SOME THORNLESS CANE FRUITS [Underscore]

Raspberry - Exceptional variety with very large berries; fruits almost continuously from July to Nov.

Oregon Blackberry - Has very decorative foliage & fruits ripen in heavy clusters from Sept. to Oct.

Loganberry - Grows very vigorously, with large berries up to 2" in length. Fruit ripens from July to August.

Youngberry - A cross between the loganberry & the blackberry. Attractive fruits wh are dark purple when mature in July & August.

[YOUNGBERRY]

10   Displayed work

When typing displayed material, try to distribute it as effectively as possible in the space available. Effective display can be achieved by:

- Thoughtful use of line spacing.
- Use of capitals and/or spaced capitals for headings.
- Use of underlining for headings.
- Emboldening headings or other items, if you use an electronic typewriter.
- Selection of appropriate margins.
- Insetting items from the left and right margins, where appropriate.

The blocked style

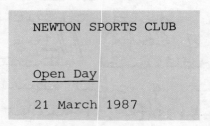

- Either begin at the left margin or centre the longest line horizontally and set the left margin at that point.
- Every line begins at the left-hand margin.
- Centre the whole piece vertically for the best effect. (See page 92 for method of vertical centring.)

The centred style

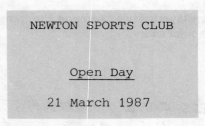

- Each line of the display is centred over the typing line.
- Use equal margins for the most effective display.
- If you use an electronic typewriter, it may have an automatic centring facility to speed up the centring task.

Complex displays

- In a complex piece of displayed work a variety of styles may be used to achieve the most effective layout.
- Where the main emphasis is on centred display, part of the work may be typed in blocked style.
- In a blocked style layout, some of the items may be centred.
- Displays containing 2 columns may be set out with the right-hand column justified at the right margin (ranged right), as in Exercise 200 on page 119.

Exercise 185   (Target time = 5 minutes)

Type the examples above.

Exercise 97

Type in the blocked style.

FOUNDATION PLANTING FOR THE GARDEN — TREES

Because trees play such a dominant role in the garden, they must be chosen very carefully. The following is a list of ones suitable for the average-sized garden.

Flowering Trees — Cherry, Almond, Laburnum, Crab Apple, Mountain Ash, Magnolia, Ornamental Plum.

Climbers & and Shrubs — Escallonia, Campsis, Broom, Clematis, Holly, Jasmine, Philadelphus, Viburnum, Rhododendron, Berberis, Lilac, Camellia, Honeysuckle, Cotoneaster, Forsythia.

ESCALLONIA

Foliage Trees — Yew, Cypress, Whitebeam, Birch

Exercise 98

Correct 2 spelling errors.

CHEESE

No one is sure how cheese was discovered, but we do no it was eaten by the Jews, Romans & Greeks several thousand yrs. ago. It was made in country farm houses & the differences in climate, soil, grass & maturity have given us the subtle differences in flavour. Some traditional English cheeses are: [Double Gloucester — a West Country cheese. [Stilton — made from summer milk & ~~is~~ at its best in Dec.
[Cheddar — made near the Cheddar Gorge for about 400 yrs.
[Derby (Sage Derby) — rare, but a favourite ~~in Dec.~~ ✓
[Cheshire — The oldest of the Eng. cheeses.
[Lancashire — once a staple food of mill workers — very good in soups and sauces]. [Wensleydale, very popular in the N. of Eng, particularly with apple. [Leicester — Is said to make the best Welsh Rarebit.

Exercise 183

Type the following invoice on an invoice form.

Typist – complete and total final column

The Manager
City Sports Store
884 Swan Road
Leeds
W Yorks LS2 9JP

Invoice No. A/1127

Your order No. D/8219

10 fishing rods, 3m @ £49.50 each
4 sets Slazenger golf clubs @ £340 each
20 boxes 'Slam' golfballs @ £15 per box
(All prices inclusive of VAT)

Exercise 184 (Target time = 20 minutes)

Type the following statement.

STATEMENT

Avon & Vestry Ltd 701 Nunnery Walk
Birmingham, B4 8NE

Telephone: Birmingham 32687

To: Woodwards Office Bureau
160 Kingston Road
CROYDON
CR9 3NQ

Date: 16 December 19--

For the month of: November

Terms: Net 30 days

Date	Ref		Debit	Credit	Balance
			£	£	£
3 Nov		Balance			342.50
7 Nov	5772	Goods	127.75		470.25
12 Nov	977	Returns		39.50	430.75
15 Nov		Cheque		300.00	130.75
21 Nov	6099	Goods	53.10		183.85

Memorandums, forms and form filling

6 Envelope addressing: business letters

Envelope addressing

Inserting envelopes

Envelopes should be inserted into the machine on the left-hand side of the cylinder. The flap should be downwards and towards the operator. The paper grips should be moved so that they are in the correct position for holding down the envelope.

Envelope sizes, folding paper for insertion into envelopes

Two commonly used sizes of envelope are C6 and C5/6. The following diagram shows how to fold A4 paper for insertion into envelopes.

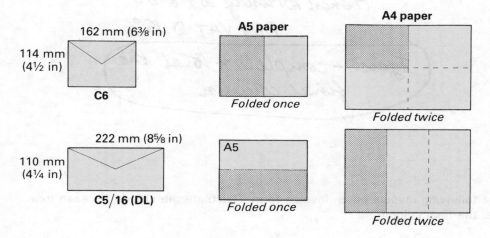

Fold paper like this to insert.
(You can also fold paper like this to make practice envelopes.)

Typing envelopes

- The full name and address should be typed parallel to the length of the envelope.
- Begin approximately half-way down the envelope.
- Begin approximately one-third in from the left edge.
- Type each line of the address on a separate line, wherever possible. If it is necessary to type the postcode on the same line as the last item of the address, leave at least 2 character spaces before typing the postcode.
- Use single-line spacing, except on large envelopes, where double-line spacing may be used.
- Type the name of the post town in capitals.
- For overseas addresses, type the name of the country in capitals.

Exercise 181 (Target time = 20 minutes)

Type the following invoice, making the necessary alterations. You may photocopy the invoice form shown on page 169.

Mr John Webster
 Manager
Royal Hotel
Brighton,
Sussex, BN1 0YN

Invoice No. 7462

Date

Your order No. B/4781

			£
10 Bottles Spanish Wine @ £2·84 each			28·40
12 " Sherry (Dry) @ £3·19 "			
10 " Italian Red Wine @ £2·68 "			
5 " Ruby Port @ £3·93 "			
6 " Malt Whiskey @ £8·96 "			
10 " Dry Gin @ £8·51 "			
10 " French Brandy @ £8·65 "			
Plus VAT @ 15%			

Typist – complete & total the final column

Exercise 182 (Target time = 25 minutes)

Type the following invoice on an invoice form. Calculate the charge for each item and total the final column.

Invoice No. 247681
Your order No. 8761
To: Mrs. A. Jamieson, Abercrombie House, Arbroath, Scotland.
27 Jan. 19-- 6 yds. Pattern no. 7. 9 ft. wide broadloom
All wool carpet (18 sq. yds.) @ £8.95 per sq. yd.,
8 yds. Pattern no. 4 plain twist pile 27 in. wide
(6 sq. yds) @ £9.95 per sq. yd., 5 pure wool rugs,
Style A (large size) @ £20.25 ea., 6 pure wool rugs,
Style B (small size) @ £18. each. 6 yds. 12ft wide
(24 sq. yds.) foam-based tufted pile @ £6.85 per sq. yd.,
5 yds. 6 ft wide (10 sq. yds.) wool shag pile, foam-based,
@ £8.95 per sq. yd. (All prices include VAT).

- The postcode should always be the last item in the address for British addresses. Where space is short, you may type the postcode on the same line as the last item of the address, whether this is the post town, the county or the country, leaving at least 2 clear character spaces before typing the postcode. Always leave 1 clear space between the two parts of the postcode, and do not type a full stop after it, even if you are using full punctuation.
- Where the postcode is included in the address it is not essential to include the name of the county. If the postcode is not included you should add the name of the county (with the exception of a few large cities, listed in the *Post Office Guide*). A number of county names may be typed in abbreviated form, and these are listed in the *Post Office Guide*. Exercises 153-155 give more information on this aspect of typing addresses.

Courtesy titles   The correct courtesy title should always be used with a person's name:

```
Mrs Kay Brown          Ms G K A Quinn
Mr B Johnson           Alhaji S Adejumobi
The Rev T L Barnes     Ray Vickers Esq
```

Use either Mr or Esq when addressing a man — do not use both.

Company names   Courtesy titles should not be used before the name of a limited company, eg, *John Brown & Co Ltd, Oduna Enterprises Ltd,* or *The Graham Manufacturing Company PLC.* Some people like to use the title 'Messrs' before the name of a partnership, such as *Messrs Smith, Jukes & Patel,* but this is not considered essential nowadays.

Special instructions   Special instructions concerning postage or delivery may be typed on the envelope, as shown below:

REGISTERED, RECORDED DELIVERY, FIRST CLASS, AIRMAIL, etc	Type in capitals in the top left-hand corner of the envelope.
PERSONAL, CONFIDENTIAL, URGENT, etc	Type in capitals as the first item of the address. Turn up twice to leave 1 clear line space before the name and address.
Attention line eg, FOR THE ATTENTION OF MR G W BILBY	Type as the first item of the address, in capitals, or in lower case with initial capitals and underscore. Turn up twice to leave 1 clear line space before typing the address.

'Window' envelopes   Where these are used, the inside address on the letter itself must be typed in a particular position so that it comes within the limits of the transparent or open window when it is folded and inserted into the envelope. The space for the address is usually marked by a box or other indication on the letter-headed paper to help the typist. When the folded letter is inserted into the envelope, ensure that any special instructions such as PERSONAL or FOR THE ATTENTION OF MR C JONES are clearly visible. Instructions concerning postage, such as FIRST CLASS, will still need to be typed on the envelope in the top left-hand corner.

Invoices and statements

In most business situations today, a printed form is used for invoices and statements. The filling in of such a form on the typewriter calls for no greater skill than that required on other pre-printed forms dealt with earlier in this section. The rapidly increasing use of either mechanised or computerised accounting systems has reduced the number of occasions when a typist is required to type an invoice or statement, in all but the smallest of businesses.

VAT (value added tax) In the United Kingdom, VAT is added to most goods. A separate column may be used to show VAT and the typing of this column should be consistent with the other columns.

- Set tabular stops at the appropriate points for each column.
- Single-line spacing is generally used.
- It is easiest to block columns below the printed headings.
- Align the figures on the decimal point.

Exercise 180   (Target time = 10 minutes)

Type the following invoice. (Invoice form on page 169).

INVOICE   No.

Avon & Vestry Ltd 701 Nunnery Walk
Birmingham, B4 8NE

Telephone: Birmingham 32687

Sold to:	Woodwards Office Bureau 160 Kingston Road CROYDON CR9 3NQ		Date: 21 November 19--

Your Order No. AVC/2776   Terms: Net 30 days

Quantity	Description	Unit cost	Amount
		£	£
10 reams	A4 Superwhite typewriting paper	2.50	25.00
5 "	A4 Flimsy paper	1.95	9.75
8 "	A5 White bank paper	2.25	18.00
20 "	A4 Special duplicating paper	2.40	48.00
			100.75
	Plus VAT @ 15%		15.12
	Total due		£115.87

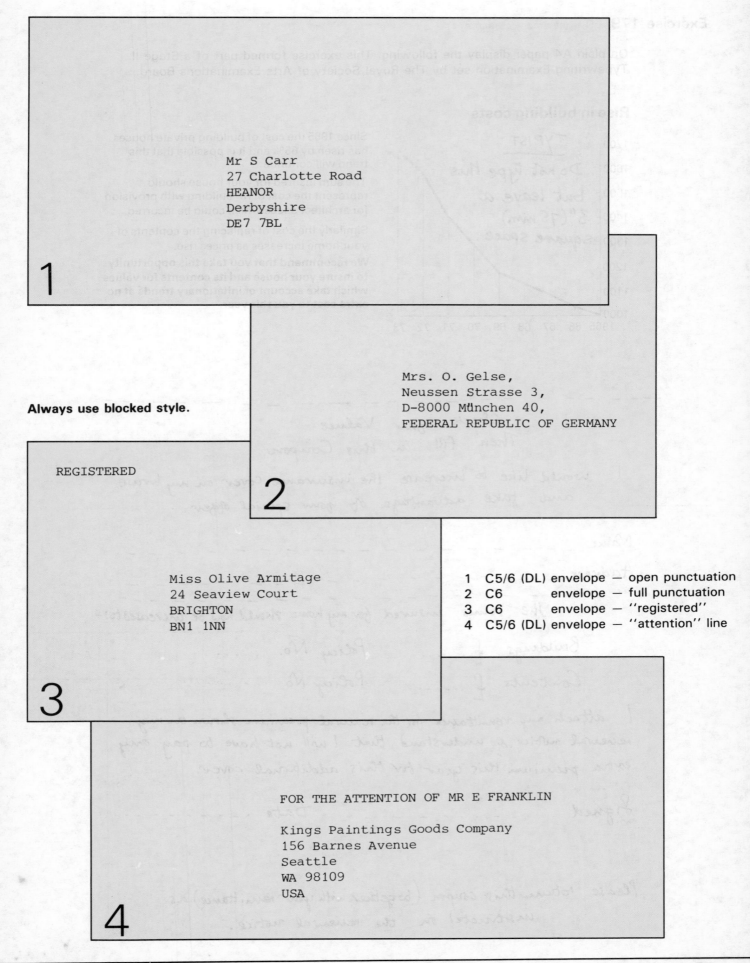

1

Mr S Carr
27 Charlotte Road
HEANOR
Derbyshire
DE7 7BL

Always use blocked style.

2

Mrs. O. Gelse,
Neussen Strasse 3,
D-8000 München 40,
FEDERAL REPUBLIC OF GERMANY

3

REGISTERED

Miss Olive Armitage
24 Seaview Court
BRIGHTON
BN1 1NN

1   C5/6 (DL) envelope — open punctuation
2   C6   envelope — full punctuation
3   C6   envelope — ''registered''
4   C5/6 (DL) envelope — ''attention'' line

4

FOR THE ATTENTION OF MR E FRANKLIN

Kings Paintings Goods Company
156 Barnes Avenue
Seattle
WA 98109
USA

Exercise 179 <small>(Target time = 25 minutes)</small>

On plain A4 paper display the following. This exercise formed part of a Stage II Typewriting Examination set by The Royal Society of Arts Examinations Board.

Rise in building costs

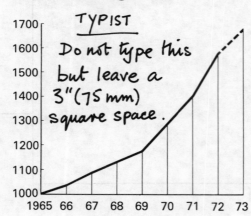

TYPIST

Do not type this but leave a 3" (75 mm) square space.

Since 1965 the cost of building private houses has risen by 65% and it is possible that this trend will continue.

The sum insured for your house should represent the cost of re-building with provision for architect's fees which could be incurred.

Similarly the cost of replacing the contents of your home increases as prices rise.

We recommend that you take this opportunity to insure your house and its contents for values which take account of inflationary trends at no extra cost to you this year.

- -

Check your Values
Then fill in this Coupon

I would like to increase the insurance cover on my house and take advantage of your special offer

Name -

Address -
- -

The sums insured for my home should now be increased to:-

Buildings £ ....   Policy No. ....
Contents £ ....   Policy No ....

I attach my remittance for the renewal premium shown on my renewal notice & understand that I will not have to pay any extra premium this year for this additional cover.

Signed - - - - - - - - -   Date - - - - - - - - -

Please return this coupon (together with your remittance) as instructed on the renewal notice.

Memorandums, forms and form filling   **110**

When envelopes are not available to you for practice purposes, fold some sheets of paper to the various sizes for typing the following exercises (see page 55).

Exercise 99

Type the following on C6 envelopes using open punctuation. Type the overseas addresses as shown with the name of the country in capitals.

Sidney Carter, MA, 14 Church Lane, Gloucester GL1 2NF
The Carlton Furnishing Co Ltd, 135 Adelaide Street West, Toronto 9, Canada,
FOR THE ATTENTION OF MISS J CONRAD
Miss Susan Jones, 'Windyridge', 29 Derry Road, Exeter, Devon, EX1 1LD
PRIVATE AND CONFIDENTIAL, Messieurs Roberts et Roberts, 26 Boulevard de la
Patrie, Paris 15e, France
Baptist World Alliance, 1628 Sixteenth Street, NW, Washington, DC 20009, USA

Exercise 100

Type the following on C5/6 envelopes, using open punctuation.

Registered, Mr William Fern, 'Wynwood', 46 Eastwood Drive, Preston, Lancs,
PR1 4JJ
M Jean Petrie, 16 Rue Joseph II, 118 Brussels, Belgium
James Smith (Nigeria) Ltd, PO Box 210, 4 Kofo Abayomi, Apapa, Lagos, Nigeria
RECORDED DELIVERY
The Rt Hon Robert Drummond, 'Avoca', Denby Place, Bristol BS2 4BO

For the attention of Mrs R Phillips, Pitman Publishing Corporation,
    6 East 43 Street, New York, NY 10017, USA
The Secretary, Sharp Tools Ltd, Hecla Works, Brightside Road, Sheffield,
    South Yorks, S1 1WJ
Messrs Howard & Jones, Royal Chambers, 15 Church Square, Cardiff,
    Wales, CF1 4EP
Urgent, The Manager, Scottish Kilt & Tartan Co. Ltd, 19 Crombie Street,
    Edinburgh, Scotland, EH1 4DS
Sig Mario Martucci, Via Conte Rosso 12, Rome, Italy
D L Harrison & Co Ltd, Palace Buildings, Grosvenor Hill,
    London W2X 5ER

Exercise 101

Type the following on C5/6 envelopes, using either full punctuation or open punctuation.

The Rev Arthur King, The Manse, Dereham, Norfolk
Pitman Publishing Ltd, PO Box 46038, Banda Street, Nairobi, Kenya
Sr Carlos Cremata, Florida 137, Buenos Aires, Argentine Republic
PERSONAL Adrian Brown, Jun, 36 Graham Road, Leeds, West Yorks LS1 6LU
Vladimir Pavel & Co Ltd, Thunovska ulice 29, Prague, Czechoslovakia

Draft a form for office use from the information given.

JOINT STAFF PENSION FUND

Complete this form   PENSION NUMBER — — — — —

(Please type or print in block letters) It will be ack.
by the return of the ~~dup.~~ tear-off slip which you
should keep. If this slip is not ret. to you
within 4 weeks, please write to the Secretary.

I Inform^n on Participant

[Typist]

put in headings for Surname, First name,
Sex, nationality, marital status ~~m.~~ date of
birth.

Cap. ___ II Inf. on wife and children under
21 yr. of age.

WIFE Name ___ — Date of birth — — —
        address — Date of marriage — — — —

                Names   Sex   date of birth

Children ___ — — — — — — — —

        III Declaration
   I declare that the above inform^n is complete, true
and accurate to the best of my knowledge
   date ———————   Signature ————
            JOINT STAFF P — F —
Name of member — — —   Pension number — — — —
Receipt of Registration Form dated — — — — — . is
hereby acknowledged.
(date) ——————   — — — Secretary

Business letters

Letterheaded paper

Business letters are typed on special stationery which has a printed heading showing the name of the company, firm or individual, the address and telephone number, the telex and telegraphic addresses, and any other information currently required by law or desired by the company concerned. Many firms also like to print their 'logo' on the letterheaded paper — this is a symbol used on all their products and advertising material to identify the company quickly and easily. An example of A4 letterheaded paper is shown on page 167 and of A5 letterheaded paper on page 168. These may be photocopied for use with the exercises in this book.

If you are not able to photocopy the headed paper for use with exercises, use plain paper of the appropriate size. Leave 9 spaces on A5 paper and 12 spaces on A4 paper to allow for the space that would be taken up by the printed heading.

Layout

There are two main styles of layout for business letters in current use: the **blocked style** and the **indented style**. The indented style may also be called the 'displayed' style. Examples of the two styles of layout are shown on pages 60-61, 66-68 and 74-76, and you should study the requirements of each style carefully.

There are several variations of these layouts, and you may find that the 'house-style' of your employer is different. You should, of course, follow the house-style used in your office.

Line spacing

Leave at least one clear space (consistently) between each part of the letter, ie, turn up 2 spaces. For a very short letter, leave 2 or 3 line spaces between parts of the letter (consistently). Always leave 1 clear line space between paragraphs in the body of the letter, and at least 4 line spaces for the signature space.

Margins

Align the left margin with the start of the printing of the letter heading. This should be at least 1" (25 mm) on A4 paper. Use equal margins, ie, at least 1" (25 mm) on the left and right for letters on A4 paper, and at least ½" (12 mm) for letters on A5 paper. Wider margins may be used for short letters.

Punctuation

Unless you are specifically asked to use full punctuation, you are recommended to use the open punctuation style. This means that all unnecessary punctuation is omitted: no punctuation is required other than that grammatically necessary in the body of the letter — and any punctuation appearing in the names of individuals or organisations, eg, Miss G D'Arcy, O'Neill Enterprises Limited, Mr Brian Rhys-Powell.

Parts of a letter

The various parts of a business letter are identified in Fig 1 and Fig 2. The numbers on the letter correspond with the numbered items listed on the following pages.

Circular letters

Circular letters are letters of the same content sent to a number of customers. Copies are made of the original and used as required.

Date   This may be typed: *a* as day, month, year, as for a business letter; *b* January, 19-- (month and year); *c* date as postmark.

Signature   If the letter is not to be signed, type the name of the sender with 1 clear line space above and below.

Tear-off portion   Some circular letters include a 'tear-off' reply slip. This portion should end about 1 inch (25 mm) from the bottom of the page. Any extra space should be left after the letter itself. Use the hyphen for the 'tear-off' line, typed from edge to edge of the paper. Leave at least 1 clear line space after the 'tear-off' line.

Exercise 177   (Target time = 20 minutes)

Type the following circular letter on letterheaded paper with a tear-off slip. Do not leave space for the signature.

```
Our Ref   RMC/--

Date as postmark
(Leave 9 clear spaces)
Dear
```

TEABLEND SPECIALITY TEAS

We were very pleased to receive your request for our Speciality Miniatures, & sincerely hope that you enjoyed them & found at least one to suit your taste. These samples are only representative of our total speciality range of teas – four other blends make up the total complement. [A special order form is attached to enable you to try any one of these teas without paying any more than you would for ordinary tea. I enclose a price list for all blends. [Teablend Speciality stockists in your area will be pleased to supply your order if you prefer not to order by post.

Yrs. flly R M Carr, Group Marketing Manager

```
Please supply ..... bags of ............................. tea

and invoice within 21 days.

Name   (Mr/Mrs/Miss) ..................................................

Address ...............................................................

        ...............................................................

        ...............................................................

Signature ........................... Date ...................
```

The blocked style

In this style all lines of the letter begin at the left-hand margin. Both Figures 1 and 2 are examples of this style. Use A5 letterheaded paper if possible (page 168) or leave 9 clear line spaces on plain paper to allow for the letterhead.

```
            ①
(1)  Our ref  Accts/306
            ①
(2)  2 January 19--
            ①
(4)  Mr T M Osman
     341 West Street
     YORK
     YO3 2HH
            ①
(5)  Dear Sir
            ①
(7)  Thank you for your letter of 22 December, and your
     remittance of £500.
            ①
     We are, of course, very pleased to have this, but have
     to point out to you that it is not now for the correct
     amount.  We think you have failed to notice that the
     discount we offered was subject to payment within 28
     days.
            ①
     A statement of your account is now enclosed, and we
     shall be glad if you will remit the outstanding balance
     as soon as possible.
            ①
(8)  Yours faithfully
(9)  EVERTON CROUCH

            ④


(10) M Blackman
     Chief Accountant
            ①
(11) Enc
```

Fig 1 A letter on A5 paper, blocked style.

Form letters

Form letters are used when slightly different versions of the same letter need to be prepared many times. Space is left for the details which vary on each letter. On a word processor the skeleton of the form letter can be filed on disc, recalled when needed, and completed very quickly.

Exercise 175 (Target time = 7 minutes)

Type 1 top copy and 2 carbon copies of the following form letter on A5 letterheaded paper. Use double line spacing for the body of the letter.

```
Our Ref

(Date)

(Leave 8 line spaces)

Dear

ORDER NO .................

We have received your recent order dated ...............
and hope to despatch the goods on .......................
between 10 am and 12 noon.

If this time and/or date is not convenient to you, will you
please telephone Swindon 897654 between 9 am and 5 pm so that
a suitable delivery time/date can be arranged.

Yours faithfully
```

Exercise 176 (Target time = 10 minutes)

Complete the letter form typed in Exercise 175 with the following details. Type your own name and address in the space left for addressee details.

a   Our Ref TCW/ma, today's date, Order No AT/30479 dated 2 weeks ago, (insert date), despatch in 2 weeks' time.
b   Our Ref WWM/tc, today's date, Order No 783 4099, dated 2 weeks ago, (insert date), despatch at end of next month.
c   Our Ref MA/cb, today's date, Order No A-403 X, dated 3 weeks ago, (insert date), despatch in 8 weeks' time.

Circulation slips

If several people in an organisation need to see the same document but do not need to have a copy, a circulation slip is attached, like the one shown below. Use C6 paper or fold a sheet of A5 paper in half.

```
FOR INFORMATION

Please initial and date

RMK    RMK
BAW    BaW
TBC    T.B.C.
```

If you do not have A5 letterheaded paper, leave 9 clear line spaces on plain paper to allow for the letterhead.

BMS/WJP/BS251
①
Today's date
①
(3) FOR THE ATTENTION OF MR Y W HO
①
Computer Equipment Ltd
48 First Lok Yang Road
Jurong Town
SINGAPORE 2262

Dear Sirs

(6) DATABASE COURSES

In reply to your enquiry of 12 July, I am pleased
to tell you that we have a course of the kind you
need, particulars of which are given in the enclosed
leaflet.

You will be particularly interested in the marked
paragraph of the leaflet, where there is specific
reference to the kind of courses we run on office
machines, etc.

If you can arrange to call on me during the next
three weeks, I shall welcome the opportunity of a
talk with you. Please telephone me quoting the
reference of this letter.

Yours faithfully

B Stanley
Training Manager

Enc

Fig 2   A letter on A5 paper, blocked style.

(1) Reference This usually consists of the initials of the writer of the letter and
those of the typist, eg PAW/JS, typed against the words 'Our ref'. Some
companies like the typist's initials to be shown in lower case, eg PAW/js.
Alternatively, the reference may include details of a file number, or a customer's
account number, eg, PAW/200764/Acc/JS. You should always include a reference
showing the writer's initials and your own, unless you are asked not to do so.

Exercise 174 (Target time = 20 minutes)

Type this form, following the layout indicated. This exercise formed part of a Stage II Typewriting Examination set by The Royal Society of Arts Examinations Board.

(Centre in closed caps. & u/sc.) Praxiteles Pension Fund and Life Assurance Scheme

(Centre in closed caps.) Nomination of Beneficiary

Name of Member _ _ _ _ _ _ _ _ _ _ _ _ Membership Certificate No. _ _ _ _ _

Under the terms of the above-named Pension Fund & Life Assurance Scheme, I hereby nominate the follg. persons as beneficiaries to whom the benefits payable

trs. under the Scheme are to be paid in the event of my death.

I reserve the right to cancel this nomination at any time.

1. My Wife/Husband* (full name) _ _ _ _ _ _ _ _ _ _ _

u.c. of address _ _ _ _ _ _ _ _ _ _ _ _ _

_ _ _ _ _ _ _ _ _ _ _ _ _

trs. in the event of him/her* surviving me for a period of 30 days.

2. In the event of my Wife/Husband* not surviving me for the said period of 30 days, I nominate the following:

u.c. Full name of nominee _ _ _ _ _ _ _ _ _ _ _

Address _ _ _ _ _ _ _ _ _ _ _ _ _

_ _ _ _ _ _ _ _ _ _ _ _ _

Relationship to Member (if any) _ _ _ _ _ _ _ _ _

If an existing nomination is to be cancelled,

u.c. (at left margin) please state name of former nominee _ _ _ _ _ _ _

← Signature of Member _ _ _ _ _ _ _ _ Date _ _ _ _ _ _ _

←* Delete as necessary.

← Note: This nomination does not become effective until it has been acknowledged and approved in writing by the Trustees of the Praxiteles Pension Fund & Life Assce. Scheme.

Memorandums, forms and form filling

The reference shown on any incoming letter should be included in the letter of reply against the words 'Your ref'.

Where the words 'Our ref' and 'Your ref' are printed on the letterheaded paper, take care to align the typing with the printed words and leave at least 1 space before beginning to type the reference, eg,

Our Ref   WD/mm

Your Ref   B6032/PA

(2) Date   The date must always be typed on a letter, even if you are not given instructions to include it. The date should be typed in the following order: day, month and year, with the name of the month in full, eg:

10 April 1989   4 May 1992

Leave at least 1 clear line space below the printed letterhead before starting to type (turn up 2 times).

(3) Special instructions   Any special instructions, such as PERSONAL, PRIVATE, CONFIDENTIAL, etc, should be typed above the name and address of the recipient. Leave at least 1 clear line space between the special instruction and the name and address.

Attention line   Some business organisations like all correspondence to be addressed to the company rather than to individuals. In such cases it is usual to include an 'attention line' to ensure that the letter is directed to the appropriate department or individual, eg:

FOR THE ATTENTION OF MR A JONES

FOR THE ATTENTION OF MRS B WILMOT, SALES DEPARTMENT

For the Attention of Miss R Timmings, Customer Services

The attention line may be typed in capitals, with or without the underscore, or in lower case with initial capitals and underscored.

The attention line may be typed above the name and address of the company, with at least 1 clear line space between it and the name and address. Alternatively, the attention line may be typed below the address; leave at least 1 clear line space between the address and the attention line.

(4) Inside name and address   The name and address of the individual or company to whom the letter is being sent should always be included. These details are usually typed above the salutation. Each line of the address should start at the left margin. Use single-line spacing. When typing the inside name and address, follow the guidelines given for addressing envelopes on pages 55-56.

(5) Salutation   The opening words of greeting in a letter are known as the 'salutation', and the forms used in business include the following.

Dear Sirs	Where the letter is addressed to a business
Dear Sir Dear Madam *or* Dear Mr Brown Dear Miss Wilson	Where the addressee's name appears in the inside address. (Note that the initial(s) of the person's first name(s) is not included in the salutation.)
Dear John Dear Elizabeth	Where the addressee is well-known by the writer

Form completion

- When you complete a form by typing the appropriate details on the insertion lines, ensure that the wording appears slightly above the line. The lower part of letters such as p and j should not touch the line.

- Insertion details should start above the first 'dot' of the insertion line. However, where a 'block' of details is to be inserted, eg, 'Other names' and 'Home address' on the form shown in Exercise 170, the details may be blocked so that all items in a particular section of the form start at the same scale point.

- Where 3 lines are provided for the address, use all the lines provided; do not type the whole address on one line.

- Where items are to be deleted, use the capital X. Align the X carefully with the variable line spacer, so that it accurately deletes the information not required.

Exercise 171 (Target time = 20 minutes)

Complete the form typed in the previous exercise, typing in the following information.

Miss B. A. Collins (Betty Anne), I.G. 65 began on 31 May, 1985 as a Shorthand-typist in Accounts. Lives at 14 Burlington Gardens, London NW4 7JG. Father J. E. Collins same address. No telephone no. [Miss Bridget Maureen O'Riley, of 24 Bankside Rd., Esher, Surrey, KT18 9HT. (Esher 469), 2 Jan., 1963. Mother - Mrs A. O'Flanagan, lives at Wicklow House, Wicklow Street, Dublin. Joined the company as a nurse on 13 September 1985 in Personnel. [Mrs M. A. Haywood married to Mr. M. A. Haywood, both of 184 Elm Road, Hornchurch, Essex, HH9 1PW (January 9, 1961), employed as Secretary to Managing Director, & began service on ~~10 May 1985~~ 12 April, 1985. No tele. no.

A form is shown on page 170 of this book. You may photocopy this for use in the following exercises.

Exercise 172 (Target time = 8 minutes)

Using a copy of the blank form given on page 170, type in your own personal details.

Exercise 173 (Target time = 14 minutes)

Using copies of the blank form given on page 170, type in the following details:

a) Mr Robert Andrew Williams, 16 Park Street, Derby DE4 8LA, Tel 0332 74179 18 years old, apprentice electrician, likes hockey, swimming and golf. Give your name and address as referee.

b) Miss Anne Wilson, 874 Brandon Road, Exeter, Devon EX3 7RW Tel 0392 40610 17 years old, hairdresser, likes basketball, gymnastics and swimming. Give your name and address as referee.

(6) Subject heading A subject heading is sometimes used to help the reader identify the content rapidly, and to ease the problem of finding a particular letter in a correspondence file. Leave one clear line space after the salutation before typing the subject heading, which may be typed in capitals with or without the underscore, or in lower case characters with initial capitals and underscored. Leave 1 clear line space after the subject heading, before starting to type the main body of the letter.

(7) Body of the letter The 'body of the letter' consists of the paragraphs of information, or the content of the letter. Single-line spacing is most generally used for the paragraphs in the body of the letter, with a clear line space between paragraphs.

(8) Complimentary close The most commonly-used forms of complimentary close are:

```
Yours faithfully     Yours sincerely
```

'Yours faithfully' should be used where the formal salutation 'Dear Sir' or 'Dear Madam' begins the letter. Letters that start with a person's name, eg, 'Dear Mr Greene', may end with either 'Yours sincerely' or 'Yours faithfully', depending on the content of the letter.

(9) Name of firm The name of the firm or organisation is often typed after the complimentary close, in capital letters.

```
Yours faithfully
ABC MANUFACTURING COMPANY PLC
```

Some companies prefer the name of the firm to be typed below the name and/or designation.

(10) Name of signatory and/or designation The signature is, of course, handwritten by the person writing the letter, or by someone authorised to sign in his/her place. However, because it is very difficult to decipher some signatures, it is usual to type the name of the person signing the letter. Leave at least 4 clear line spaces between the complimentary close and the name of the writer to allow room for the signature.

The designation (ie, the position in the firm) of the writer may also be typed, or it may be typed instead of the writer's name. The designation should be typed immediately below the name, or at least 4 clear line spaces below the complimentary close if the name is not included.

The name and the designation may be typed in capitals or in lower case with initial capitals, eg:

```
Terrence Brown       TINA WHITESIDE
Production Manager   MARKETING EXECUTIVE
```

(11) Enclosure(s) Attention is drawn to any material to be enclosed with the letter by typing an 'enclosure notation'. Where a single item is enclosed the abbreviation 'Enc' or 'Att' should be typed at the end of the letter, at least 2 clear line spaces below the name and/or designation (or at least 6 clear line spaces below the complimentary close if there is no name/designation.

Where there are several enclosures, type 'Encs', or alternatively the number of enclosures may be indicated, eg, 'Encs – 3'. Some organisations like the nature of the enclosure to be indicated, eg, 'Enc – Production Report'.

An alternative approach is to type a symbol in the left margin at the point where the enclosure is mentioned in the text. This may consist of three hyphens ---, three full stops . . ., or three oblique strokes ///. Leave at least 1 character space between the enclosure symbols in the margin and the left margin of the letter. If you wish, you may type 'Enc' or 'Encs' at the foot of the letter in addition to the marginal symbols.

Both these methods also remind the person opening the letter to look for enclosures.

Forms

You may frequently be asked to type a form for duplication to be used by other people. You will also need to be able to type details on printed forms or on form letters that have previously been duplicated.

Displaying forms

- The form should be well-displayed on the page, not cramped up at the top of the page.
- Use 1½ or double spacing for the insertion lines.
- Paragraphs of text may be in single-line spacing.
- A justified right margin (all lines ending at the same point) can be achieved by continuing all dotted lines to the right margin, if desired.
- Lines may be typed using continuous dots or the underscore. Leave one space before typing the line.
- There may be details which begin part way across the page. To determine the point at which to type these details, estimate the amount of space likely to be required for the details to be inserted on that line.

Exercise 170 (Target time = 12 minutes)

Type the form shown below on A5 paper. Take 2 carbon copies.

```
PERSONNEL DEPARTMENT

Surname (capital letters, please) ...........................................

Other names ................................................................

Home address ...............................................................

             ...............................................................

             ................................... Postcode ..................

Telephone number ....................

Next of kin ....................... Day, month, year of birth ..............

Address ........................... Commenced Company service on ...........

        ........................... Department ............................

        ........................... Designation of post ...................
```

Exercise 102

Type Figure 1 on page 60. Type an envelope.

Exercise 103

Type Figure 2 on page 61. Use full punctuation. Type an envelope.

Exercise 104

Type the following letter on A5 paper. Use today's date.

The Manager
Charlton Hotel
Rue de Pierre
St Peter Port
Guernsey   CHANNEL ISLANDS

Dear Sir

I write to confirm my telephone booking of yesterday for two single rooms, bed and breakfast, for the two weeks commencing 8 August for the Business Equipment conference. I enclose a deposit for my colleague, Mr J Swift and myself of £20.

I will let you know nearer the date the time of our arrival at the airport.

Yours faithfully

John Newman

Enc

Exercise 105

Type the following letter on A5 paper. Type an envelope.

Mrs D. E. Dickson 24 Abercrombie Ave. Edinburgh EH9 4AH
Dear Mrs Dickson, Thank you for your recent enquiry regarding our new moisturizing cream. I have pleasure in sending you a leaflet our new descriptive leaflet, together with a small sample I hope you will enjoying using. I know hope you will be delighted with this new product in our range of cosmetics, and look forward to receiving your order very soon. Don't delay — the demand will be heavy, particularly just before Easter. Yrs. Sincerely. P. Brown, Sales Promotion Manager Encs (2)

Display the following memorandum on A4 memo-headed paper as effectively as possible. The lists of programme items may be typed in either single or double spacing. This exercise formed part of a Higher Examination set by the London Chamber of Commerce and Industry.

INTERNAL MEMORANDUM

(Typist: Please insert today's date)

FROM: Chief Producer   DATE:

TO: All programme producers   SUBJECT: Future Programmes

The following programmes will form the framework of our broadcasting schedules for the coming year. The length of each programme [will] *is to* be the same as this year. Producers of all sections (pop, classical and light music, drama, sports, comedy and games) are asked to draw up plans for two-hour periods per week in their special areas of entertainment and to have these ready for discussion at a meeting to be held in the Chief Producer's office in July. The exact date and time of the meeting will be announced next week.

HOME   7.00 News. Weather. 7.15 Commentary. 7.45 Religious talk. 8.00 News. Weather. 8.30 Light music. 9.00 News. Weather. 9.30 Schools. 12.30 Listeners' Choice. 1.00 News. Weather. 2.00 Schools. 5.00 Topical talk. 6.00 News. Weather. 8.00 From the Grass Roots. 9.00 Classical music. 10.00 News. Weather. 10.15 Stock Exchange. 10.30 Light music. 11.00 News. Weather. 11.20 Close.

OVERSEAS   7.00 World News. 7.15 Radio Newsreel. 7.45 Letter from London. 8.00 News. Weather. 8.30 As Home Service. 9.00 News. Weather. 9.30 World Theatre. 11.30 Radio Newsreel. 1.00 News. 1.10 Commentary. 2.00 Sports Desk. 3.00 Light music. 5.00 Topical talk. 6.00 News. 6.30 The World of Science. 7.30 New Books. 8.00 Light music. 10.00 News. 10.20 Close.

Exercise 106

Type the following letter on A5 paper. Insert today's date.

Mrs. Mariko Sin, Tong Chong Street, Quarry Bay, Hong Kong; Dear Mrs Sin, Will you please telephone me in connection with the dental appointment you made for your daughter last week. I regret I shall have to change this appointment for you, as Mr. O'Neil has suddenly been taken ill and is not expected to be in his surgery again for at least a month. If the treatment for your daughter is urgent, I suggest you contact Mr. Patrick Hewitt in Hennesey Road, who will no doubt be able to help you. I apologize for any inconvenience this will cause. Yours sincerely, Mary Gordon, Receptionist.

Exercise 107

Type the following letter on A5 paper.

The Rev. John Adams, D.D., The Old Vicarage, Church Road, Leicester, LE6 6FR. Dear Sir, Thank you for your inquiry regarding the installation of chiming bells at your church. I appreciate that such an expensive item as this will need to be discussed in some detail by your Parochial Church Council, and would suggest therefore that I come to see you before their next meeting. I shall be in your district next Monday and could see you then, if convenient to you. Perhaps you could let me know by telephone to save time. Yours faithfully, CHURCH BELLS (ELECTRONIC) LIMITED.

Exercise 108

Type this letter using open punctuation. Type an envelope.

9 November 19-- Our Ref. OH/5/4 - LMB/GR. Mr. L. Evans, 20 Gwyneth Road, Swansea, SW4 9DS. Dear Mr. Evans, ANNUAL CATALOGUE We regret to say that we now find it necessary to increase the price of our annual catalogue owing to because of increased printing charges, & also to the fact that six extra pages have been added. The cost is now £1.50, post free plus postage, which is still exceptionally low compared with high production costs. We trust this will not affect our longstanding, happy relationship, and look forward to hearing from you very soon. Yrs. sincerely F. W. Lewis, Sales Manager, Quantock Reproductions plc

Exercise 166 (Target time = 12 minutes)

Display the following memo on A4 paper. Take one carbon copy and make the necessary alterations. Arrange the vacancies in correct numerical order and type as blocked paragraphs.

To: Publicity Dept From: Personnel Dept. Date 12 Feb 19-- . Subject: Staff Vacancies. Will you please arrange for the following vacancies to be advertised during the next two weeks. Required immediately. for Everton Crouch ③ Telephonist (Part-time considered). Pref. GPO trained. Hours & pay by arrangement. ② Secretary. Salary from £7,500 p.a. according to experience. Electric typewriter. ① Clerk-typist & Receptionist. School-leaver considered. Some shorthand an advantage. £100 p.w. Interesting & varied work) Pleasant working conditions. Hours 9.30 - 5.30 - no Saturdays. Phone for appointment 01-968-2516. Ext 21 ④ Audio Secretary. Interesting varied work with some receptionist duties. Salary negotiable. £6,500 p.a. upwards. Good appearance and personality required for dealing with clients.

Exercise 167 (Target time = 8 minutes)

Type the following memo on A5 memo-headed paper and take one carbon copy.

Memorandum To: All Sales Representatives From: Sales Manager. 1 July 19-- Claims for Expenses Please note that expense claim forms must now be completed in duplicate and sent to reach the Accounts Department not later than the end of the first week of the month following the period for which the claim is made. Representatives are urged to comply with this new ruling in order that recently established routines relating to cash flow control may operate efficiently. If everyone concerned co-operates in making the new system work, a general improvement in settlement of claims will result.

Exercise 168 (Target time = 8 minutes)

Display the following memo on A5 paper. Take one carbon copy.

Memorandum To: All members of Staff From: Personnel Manager 1 August 19-. Private Patients' Health Care Scheme. Any staff member who is included in the Company Pension Plan is eligible to join this scheme. The Company will pay the subscription for the member and, if required, for the member's spouse. Members may also arrange cover for their children, though in this case an annual premium of £35 per child must be paid by the member. The amounts paid by the Company on behalf of the employee will be subject to income tax. Application forms and brochures describing the scheme in detail are available on request.

Check your work

Remember that you should always check your work — and try to cultivate the habit of reading what you have typed, not what you *think* or *hope* you have typed. If, when checking your own typing, you find a mistake which you cannot correct neatly or feel the work is badly positioned on the page, type the letter again. Take a pride in your work. It *must* be accurate or it is useless. It should also be pleasing to look at.

The indented style (see numbered example below)

(1) The **reference** is typed at the left-hand margin.

(2) The **date** is typed on the right, finishing level with the right-hand margin. To find the starting point, move the typing point to the right margin and backspace once for *each* letter/space in the date. Both the reference and the date are on the same line.

(3) The **subject heading** is centred on the typing line.

(4) The **first line of each paragraph** is indented — usually five pica or six elite spaces.

(5) The **complimentary close** is typed either *centred* on the writing line, or beginning at the *middle* of the writing line.

(6) & (7) The **name** of the company or organisation and the **name of the signatory and designation of the writer** of the letter are often centred on the complimentary close as below, but may be aligned with the complimentary close (see page 67) — this is the quickest method and should therefore be used unless you have instructions to centre each line.

At the beginning of each task or each day's work, set tabulator stops for all pre-determined starting points, such as paragraph indentations, date, etc.

Exercise 109

Type the example below on A5 paper.

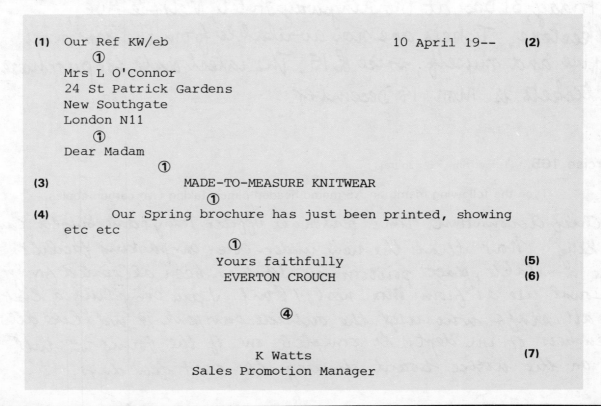

(1) Our Ref KW/eb   10 April 19--   **(2)**
          ①
Mrs L O'Connor
24 St Patrick Gardens
New Southgate
London N11
          ①
Dear Madam
                    ①
(3)   MADE-TO-MEASURE KNITWEAR
                         ①
(4)   Our Spring brochure has just been printed, showing
      etc etc
                    ①
                    Yours faithfully   **(5)**
                    EVERTON CROUCH   **(6)**

                         ④

                    K Watts   **(7)**
               Sales Promotion Manager

Envelope addressing: business letters   **66**

Exercise 163 (Target time = 8 minutes)

Type the following example and take one carbon copy. A blank memorandum form appears on page 168.

MEMORANDUM

From Head Office, London

To Leicester Branch   *Date*   1 May 19--

NEW CATALOGUES

The printers have today advised us that they will be despatching copies to
all branches at the end of this week. Please advise us if you do not
receive the number of copies you ordered within the next ten days. I
enclose a copy of the index.

TW/LD

Enc

Exercise 164 (Target time = 8 minutes)

Type the following memo on A5 memo-headed paper and take one carbon copy.

To: All members of Staff. From: Social Secretary. New Year Celebration Party. The New Year Celebration Party will be held on Friday, 31 Dec, at the Kingsway Hotel, Melrose Ave., Folkestone. Tickets are now available from the Personnel Office and myself, price £15. The latest date for purchase of tickets is Mon. 18 December.

Exercise 165 (Target time = 8 minutes)

Type the following memo on A5 memo-headed paper, taking two carbon copies.

To: Chief Accountant From: Personnel Officer. Today's date, Subject: Car Parking. Now that the new under-cover car parking facilities are available, platt position no. 34 has been allocated for yr. personal use as from Mon. next, 1 April. I am compiling a list of all staff who uses the outside car park, & wd. like all members of yr. dept. to complete one of the forms wh. will be on the notice board during the next few days.

Memorandums, forms and form filling

Exercise 110

Type the following example on A5 letterheaded paper.

The
indented
style on
A5 paper

Our Ref KW/eb   10 April 19--

Mrs L O'Connor
24 St Patrick Gardens
New Southgate
London N11

Dear Madam

                    MADE-TO-MEASURE KNITWEAR

        Our Spring brochure has just been printed,
showing a most colourful and wide variety of made-
to-measure clothes which we are sure will interest
you.

        We do not seem to have heard from you for some
time now, but as we do not wish to remove your name
from our mailing list, we are giving you another
opportunity to obtain a copy of our exciting brochure.

        Stocks are limited, so be sure to send us your
name and address today, and you will receive our brochure without delay. Act now to avoid disappoinment
- we have some wonderful bargains!

                    Yours faithfully
                    EVERTON CROUCH

                    K Watts
                    Sales Promotion Manager

Compli-
mentary
close —
each line
begins at
the centre
of the
page

Envelope addressing: business letters   **67**

9 Memorandums, forms and form filling

Memorandums

Day-to-day communication between departments or branches of an organisation is generally by typewritten memorandums which are much simpler and therefore quicker to type than a letter. Many organisations have their own printed memorandum forms. Where there are no such forms, you will be expected to use plain paper, either A5 (used landscape) or, for longer memos, an A4 sheet. There is no one standard form of layout for a memorandum because it varies from organisation to organisation as much as business letterheadings.

A sample memo-headed form is shown on page 168. You may photocopy this for use with the exercises in this book.

Margins At least 1″ (25 mm). Align with the printed words in the heading on the left side and use a corresponding right margin.

Date Typed as in letters. Always include the date, even if you are not instructed to do so.

Printed headings Align your typing with the bottom of the printed words. Leave 2 clear spaces before typing the insertions. The variable line spacer (see page 3) is used to align your typing with the printed words. The line on the transparent paper holder indicates the bottom of the typing line.

Subject headings Usually typed in capitals.

Reference If there is not a printed 'Ref', type the reference either above the date or at the foot of the memo, as shown in the example on page 101. Leave at least one clear line space, more if the memo is to be initialled or signed.

Enclosure If there is an enclosure, indicate as in letters (see page 63).

Spacing Normally, single spacing is used, with a clear line space between paragraphs.

Continuation sheet If a memorandum continues on to a second page, type the following continuation details at the top of the sheet; 'From' and 'To' details as shown on the first page, the date in the same position as on the first page and the page number. The page number may be centred above the other continuation details on a line of its own.

Exercise 111

Type the following example on A5 letterheaded paper.

Our Ref Cat/101/DFE   22 May 19--
①
FOR THE ATTENTION OF MR KAMI SIDA

Continental Hotel
210 Main Street
San Fernando
Trinidad
WEST INDIES

Dear Sirs

               Deep-Freezing Equipment

        Thank you for your inquiry of last week for
details of our deep-freezing equipment.

        We are now able to send you our latest cata-
logue showing the different models that are available, with all the relevant information to help you
make up your mind which type of freezer is most
appropriate for your hotel. The back page of the
catalogue tells you all you need to know about
insurance.

        Should you require any further information,
our representative will be pleased to call on you.

                    Yours sincerely

                    R Mason

Enc

Note the
position of
the
attention
line

Note the
position of
Enc.

Type the following letter on A4 headed paper making any necessary corrections, and take one carbon copy.

Ref. 2153
Mr. A Cuthbertson, 125a Hewitts Road Shrewsbury
Shropshire SY3 8NX

Dear Mr. Cuthbertson,

<u>Staff Association</u>

Thank you for your cheque for £10.50 representing one year's subscription for membership of this Assocn. I enclose your membership card, together with a booklet relating to goods & services which can be obtained at reduced prices by members. We hope that the benefits you will enjoyed by belonging to this Assocn. will influence you to encourage any of your associates who have not yet become members to join, and so enable further funds to be available for extended club facilities. You will see from the following table how increased membership gives additional benefits to all members.

	1985	1986
No. of members	1,000	1,500
Income from investments, subscriptions + fund-raising activities	£3,000	£6,500
Amount spent on members' welfare (sports pavilion, re-furnished club room, children's party, annual dinner subsidy etc)	£2,600	£6,200

Yours sincerely
Social Secretary.

Exercise 112

Type the following letter on A5 letterheaded paper in the indented style. Use today's date. Type an envelope.

Our Ref. 290/FBw/26-104

①

Mrs. Joan King,
46 Warwick Avenue,
Newcastle-upon-Tyne.
NE29 2AL

Dear Madam,

①

INV/416/NE

①

    We regret having to remind you that the settlement of your account is now two months overdue.

①

      We feel that this is an oversight on your part, and would be glad to receive your cheque in full settlement by return of post.

①

Yours faithfully,
EVERTON CROUCH

④

Accounts Department

Exercise 113

Type the following letter on A5 letterheaded paper in the indented style. Use full punctuation. Type an envelope.

Ref. Staff File No. 36. 25 November, 19-- Mr. P. W. Atkinson, Brentwood, 92 Albany Drive, Milton Keynes, MK7 6AB. Dear Mr. Atkinson, Thank you for your letter of inquiry regarding part-time lecturing in our Training Department. I should like to enter your name on our ~~Fete~~ Staff File, & enclose the necessary application form for you to complete. Please be sure to include full partics. of all your previous teaching experience (if any) & qualifications. Please return the completed form to me. Yours sincerely, Alex Hogan, Training Manager

Exercise 159 (Target time = 20 minutes)

Type the following letter with tabular statement.

The Midland Plastic Supply Co., 49 Berwick Road, Nottingham, NG7 7FE. Dear Sirs, Thank you for your quotation and for the generous supply of samples, which are well up to our expectations. As our customers have asked for prompt delivery, please forward immediately: Table Cloths, Pattern No. 4XY, 200 @ £50 per 100, Pattern No. 6YZ, 150 @ £60 per 100. Carrier Bags, Quality A 300 @ £18 per 100, Quality B 450 @ £20 per 100. We will arrange for collection at this end and shall be obliged if you will consign the goods to St. Pancras Station, and tell us as soon as possible of the date and time of arrival. Yours faithfully, J.D. Rhodes, Buyer, EVERTON CROUCH.

Exercise 160 (Target time = 20 minutes)

Type the following letter with tabular statement.

Ref. MAB/FRT. Messrs. H. R. Siddall & Sons Ltd., 196 Martin Road, Croydon, Surrey, CR8 5BA. For the attention of the Sales Manager. Dear —, Trial Order No. 20491   With reference to your recent advertisement, please forward to this address the following items: 1 Bathroom Cabinet (white) No. 262 @ £7, 1 Bathroom Stool (white) No. 21 @ £5, 1 Shower Unit No. 346 @ £70 (complete). Please send these items as quickly as possible as they are required as samples for the Christmas trade. Yours faithfully.

Exercise 161 (Target time = 25 minutes)

Type the following letter with tabular statement.

Ref. 205/LB/AMP. C. R. Stevenson, Esq., A.M.I.C.E., North-East Construction Co. Ltd., Landsdowne Road, Bristol BS6 9OD. Dear —, With reference to your inquiry, I would like to give you the following information regarding Polythene Tubing B.S. 1973. Class A. Rate of Pressure 150 ft./head: 92.5 lb./sq.in. Class B. Rate of Pressure 200 ft./head: 150.0 lb./sq.in. Class C. Rate of Pressure 200 ft./head: 130.0 lb./sq.in. Class D. Rate of Pressure 350 ft./head: 190.0 lb./sq.in. This tubing is used very effectively in many industrial installations, particularly for the conveyance of corrosive liquids, food products, acids, alkalis, etc. Many local authorities and water boards are adopting it for use on large housing estates because it reduces labour and material costs and will not burst in extreme cold weather conditions. It is a low-density tubing and is manufactured to British Standards Specification 1973 which guarantees that it is completely dependable and consistently passes the necessary tests periodically laid down in the specification. If you would like any further details, I will be pleased to give them or, alternatively, our Technical Service Adviser, Mr. James Coombes, will call on you at any time to suit your convenience. You are also welcome to visit our factory at any time to see the tubing in use. Yours faithfully, P. Dewhurst, Technical Sales Manager.

Exercise 114

Type the following letter in the indented style. Insert today's date. Type an envelope.

Our Ref. MW/Medical 409, Private and Confidential. Dr. Elizabeth Wilson, 100 Abbey Road, Phoenix, A285026, USA. Dear Dr. Wilson, Mrs. Jean Smith This is just to confirm that the above-named patient was re-admitted to this hospital yesterday with a recurrence of her depressive phases. Mr. Lewis, our Consultant, has recommended a further short course of E.C.T., which will commence tomorrow. Mrs. Smith should have no injections at this stage of the treatment. I will report on her progress in due course and anticipate her being in hospital no more than a week. Yours sincerely, R J K Bishari, Psychotherapy Department.

Exercise 115

Retype Exercise 114 using the blocked style.

Exercise 116

Type the following letter in the indented style on A5 paper. Insert today's date. Type an envelope.

Our Ref. TWA/Medical 102. Dr. T. W. Adams, 96 Johnstone Avenue, Birmingham, B15 9WQ. Dear Dr. Adams, Re Mr. John Holland. I confirm that the above-named patient is suffering from rheumatoid arthritis in his hands and feet. I am suggesting wax baths twice daily, followed by extension exercises and the use of the pulleys and the isodyne machine. Mr. Holland should report to this hospital on Monday next to make arrangements for his treatment to commence as soon as possible. I will arrange for an ambulance to pick him up at 1100 hours. Yours sincerely, F. C. Davies, Physiotherapy Department.

Exercise 117

Type this letter on letterheaded paper using the indented style. Type an envelope.

11 March, 19-- Our Ref. LST/FR2/3. URGENT Mr T. Jackson, 42 Park Avenue, Salford, M6 9EL. Dear Mr Jackson, your letter dated 26 Feb. has only just reached us. We very much regret the shipping error and on investigation find that one of the shipping clerks did not understand the order, and as a result, shipped only part of it. We have now given instrns. for the remainder of the materials to be shipped at once, and every care will be taken to see that nothing like this ever happens again. Please accept our most sincere apologies for all the inconvenience caused. Yrs. sincerely, Sales Manager

Exercise 157 (Target time = 15 minutes)

Type a copy of this letter on headed paper with full punctuation.

Mr. A. Gibson,
Excel Service Station,
Grosvenor Road,
BIRMINGHAM B9 5UT

Dear Mr. Gibson,

I can deliver to you monthly the following car accessories at the prices quoted below, less a discount of 10 per cent:

Head Rests	£8.50	Car Radios	£20.95
Radio Aerials	£8.15	Fog Lamps	£7.55
Roof Racks	£19.00	Spot Lamps	£8.20

Alternatively, if you collect from us, the discount will be 12½ per cent.

Yours sincerely,

Manager

Exercise 158 (Target time = 15 minutes)

Type the following letter on headed paper with open punctuation.

Mrs B. Knight
Takapuna
182-190 Wairau Road
Auckland 9
NEW ZEALAND

Dear Mrs Knight,

I give below details of the timetable concerning the 10-week Refresher Secretarial Course due to commence at this College on 20 September.

Monday	9.30 - 11.00	Typewriting
	11.00 - 12.00	Shorthand
Wednesday	9.30 - 10.30	Shorthand
	10.30 - 12.30	Typewriting
Friday	9.30 - 10.30	Office Practice
	10.30 - 11.30	Typewriting
	11.30 - 12.30	Shorthand

Enrolment for this Course will take place in Room 204 on Tuesday 14 September and the Course Fee is NZ$60.50.

Yours sincerely

Principal

Carbon copies and photocopying

It is essential for later reference to keep an exact copy of all business letters, invoices and other important documents that are sent out. Copies must therefore be taken before these documents are despatched. The two most common methods of taking copies are carbon copying and photocopying.

Carbon copying

- Carbon copying is still very widely used and you should frequently take at least one carbon copy of your exercises, to become familiar with the handling of carbon paper and filing-copy paper.
- Carbon paper, or carbon-coated plastic sheets, are manufactured in various colours and sizes.
- The maximum number of copies that may be taken at one operation by means of carbon paper varies according to the thickness of the typewriting paper used, but may be from five to eight good copies if the thin paper specially manufactured for carbon copying is used.
- Care should be taken not to crease the carbon sheets, as the crease may mark the copies; this is known as 'treeing'. The carbon sheets should occasionally be turned from top to bottom, so as to use all the carbonized surface. They should not be folded or rolled, but kept flat in a special box or drawer, preferably in a cool place.

Arranging the papers   Lay a sheet of flimsy copy paper on the desk and place on it the printed letterheading, face upwards. Insert these sheets into the typewriter so that the carbon side of the sheet faces the platen. If you need to take several carbon copies, make up a 'pack' by laying down the flimsy copy paper, carbon paper (carbon side down), copy paper, carbon paper, and so on until you have enough copies, then add the final top sheet or paper or letterheaded paper. You may need to release the paper-release lever to allow you to insert the 'pack' behind the platen; return the paper-release lever and turn the platen to roll the pack of papers and carbon sheets through. If necessary, adjust the papers so that they are all evenly aligned. When several copies are being taken, strike the keys with rather more force than for ordinary single copies with a manual typewriter, or use the touch-control adjustment for electric and electronic typewriters.

Making corrections   If a mistake is made, the eraser should not be used in the ordinary way, as this would cause a smudge to appear on each carbon copy. The method of making corrections is as follows. Turn the platen forward or backward until the word to be corrected is in the right position to allow the insertion of a piece of stiff card behind the writing paper, and rest each sheet separately on this card while the erasures are made. Then return the platen to the printing point and type the necessary corrections. Make the erasure with gentle circular movements, removing all dust from the typewriter or use matching colour paint-out fluid.

If the papers have been taken out of the machine before the error is discovered, the mistake should be removed with an eraser or with a fluid corrector, then each sheet should be separately inserted into the typewriter and the correction made. A small piece of carbon paper may be placed between the ribbon and the paper to secure uniformity in the appearance of the carbon copies.

Distribution of carbon copies   When copies are to be sent to persons in addition to the main addressee, it is usual to type the abbreviation 'cc', followed by the name(s) of the other recipient(s) at the foot of a letter (one clear space below the last line).

- This note may appear on the top copy and all carbon copies so that all recipients know who has received a copy.
- If the writer does not wish all recipients to know who has received a copy, the carbon copy details are omitted from the top copy and 'bcc', followed by the name(s) of the other recipient(s), is typed on the copies only.

Money in columns

- Always use the decimal point, followed by two digits, unless all the amounts in the columns are in whole units.
- The currency symbol (eg £) may be typed at the top of all money columns.
- In the centred style, if the column is to contain the decimal point and following digits, the £ symbol when used as a heading should appear immediately above the decimal points. If it contains only whole numbers of monetary units, then the unit sign should be centred on the longest line in the column.
- In the blocked style the sign should be typed over the first unit in the column (or the monetary sign eg £ if there is one).
- The underscore should be used for the rulings at the foot of cash columns with a total. Type the first line without turning up the paper (or you may leave one line space if you prefer); then, two line spaces below, type the total. Turn up the paper one line space before typing the bottom line. The total lines should extend from the first figure in the column total to the last figure in the column. Do not underline the £ sign.
- If you wish to use the double underscore below the total, type the bottom line then use the interliner to turn up slightly to type the second line.

Exercise 156 (Target time = 15 minutes)

Type the following letter in the blocked style using open punctuation.

```
Mrs E Carter
26 Ridgeway Road
HARROW
HA1 2HA

Dear Madam

In reply to your inquiry, we list below the prices of the carpets of the
make and type you require:

LENGTH    WIDTH    FIRST QUALITY    SECOND QUALITY

m         m        £                £

4         3.250    98.15            94.60
4         3.500    99.20            96.10
5         3.000    105.25           100.65

                   £302.60          £291.35


We offer a free fitting service which includes underlay and look forward
to receiving your order.

Yours faithfully



Sales Manager
```

● The 'distribution list' is the list of names of the people receiving copies of a document. The copy to be sent to each individual should be indicated by 'ticking' or underlining the appropriate name on each copy with a coloured pen. The file copy should be identified by writing 'F' or 'File' in the top right-hand corner.

Photocopying

A photocopier will produce an identical copy of an original document in moments. In many offices it is considered quicker and more economical to take a photocopy of a letter for the file, or for distribution, than to take carbon copies. In addition there is the advantage that the copy is identical to the original.

Production typing

Production typing is the term used to indicate the amount of time taken by a typist to produce a given document. A typist should be able to produce an accurate, well-presented document in the shortest time possible. Follow the routine suggested below:

1 Carefully place *all* the necessary stationery neatly on your desk, or in the desk drawer, including envelopes and carbon paper.
2 Read quickly through the task and use your dictionary to check any spellings.
3 Highlight any special instructions regarding layout, and check through the document to ensure that punctuation, layout, etc, are consistent.
4 Make a note of any items which *you* may be required to insert, eg, the date on letters, enclosures, references, etc.
5 Decide on the size of paper to be used; check whether you need a carbon copy.
6 Decide on the most suitable margins and line spacing to be used.
7 Set tabular stops for indentation, if required.

Target times

Suggested target times are shown for the exercises that follow. You should aim to complete your work within the target time given. If you find that you are not able to achieve the suggested target time, analyse the way you work to see whether you can improve your production speed.

Decision making

In some of the exercises which follow, you will not be given full instructions and will be expected to insert the appropriate information.

Exercise 118

Type the following.

DECISION MAKING — POINTS TO REMEMBER

Insert the date on which you type the letter.
Insert a reference showing the writer's initials and your own, where the writer's name is given.
Insert the salutation if this is not given, as appropriate to the letter.
Insert an appropriate complimentary close, where this is not given, using either 'Yours faithfully' or 'Yours sincerely' as appropriate.
Include the enclosure notation where appropriate.
Take a carbon copy for each letter.
Type an envelope for each letter.

For these 3 exercises, see note on page 94 (continuous matter with tables).

Exercise 153 (Target time = 15 minutes)

Type the following in three columns, using the blocked style, and arrange alphabetically.

The Omission of County Names (1) Scotland

1. The County Name may be omitted from postal addresses in the following cities &^post towns - Inverness Shetland Lanark Glasgow Ayr Banff Clackmannan Dundee Orkney Peebles Selkirk Stirling Dumfries Dumbarton Aberdeen Kinross Nairn Renfrew Perth Kirkcudbright Edinburgh

Exercise 154 (Target time = 20 minutes)

Type the following in four columns, using the centred style, and arrange alphabetically.

The Omission of County Names (2) England & Wales

The County names may be omitted from postal addresses in the following cities and post towns - Cambridge Berwick-on-Tweed Hereford Lancaster Manchester Southampton York Worcester Peterborough Oxford Hertford Gloucester Durham Cardiff Bristol Chester Bedford Birmingham Sheffield Buckingham Nottingham Stafford Warwick Derby Leeds Liverpool Lincoln Newcastle upon Tyne Northampton Leicester

Exercise 155 (Target time = 20 minutes)

Type the following in three columns using the blocked style. Arrange alphabetically.

The Omission of County Names (3) Miscellaneous

The County name may be omitted from postal addresses in the following (post towns) & cities &^, provided the correct postcode is used.

Swansea Walsall Slough Hounslow Huddersfield Torquay Redhill Falkirk Crewe Bolton Carlisle Bath Brighton Exeter Colchester Luton Hull Ipswich Twickenham Wolverhampton Plymouth Oldham Milton Keynes Chelmsford Sunderland Warrington Salford Bournemouth Watford Preston Portsmouth Dartford Coventry Stoke-on-Trent Salisbury Blackpool Croydon Romford Swindon Southend-on-Sea Norwich Reading Blackburn Bromley Shrewsbury

Exercise 119 (Target time = 8 minutes)

Type the following letter in the blocked style using open punctuation. Take carbon copies as necessary.

Mr. T. Black, 146 Seymour Road, Portsmouth, POQ 7TH. Dear ———, Thank you for your letter of 5 July which I have only just received. I have now looked into the question of the error made in the VAT calculation on our invoice and find that you are quite right. This should read £20·50 and not £22·50, as originally stated. I do apologize for this mistake and enclose an amended invoice and shall be pleased to receive your cheque for the new amount as soon as convenient, particularly as the invoice is dated 31 May. Yours ——— Everton Crouch W. Wilkins, Manager, cc M Samuels

Exercise 120 (Target time = 15 minutes)

Refer to Exercise 119. Reply to the letter sent by Mr W. Wilkins, who works for EVERTON CROUCH — address on letterheading on page 167. Thank him for amending the invoice and say that you are enclosing a cheque — state the amount. Use plain paper.

Exercise 121 (Target time = 8 minutes)

Type the following letter in the indented style with full punctuation.

Mr. James McKinlay, 24 Keswick Drive, Lancaster, LA6 2DR. Dear ———, On looking through our records recently, we notice that you have not increased the insurance on your property since you bought it six years ago. We imagine this is merely an oversight on your part as we are sure you are aware of the rising value in houses. If you would like to discuss the matter, we should be happy to send one of our representatives to see you. Yours faithfully, F. W. Davies Manager, Accident Department. bcc M Grant, Area Representative

Exercise 122 (Target time = 15 minutes)

Refer to Exercise 121. Ask Mr Davies, who works for Everton Crouch, if he can arrange for a representative to call as soon as possible. Mr McKinlay would, of course, like him to telephone to arrange a convenient time. Use plain paper.

Envelope addressing: business letters

Exercise 151 (Target time = 10 minutes)

Type the following, in the blocked style.

THE LARGEST NATIONS OF THE WORLD

Country	Population (millions)
Bangladesh	95
Brazil	119
China	1 008
Federal Republic of Germany	61
India	685
Indonesia	153
Italy	57
Japan	119
Mexico	67
Nigeria	82
Pakistan	83
United Kingdom	55
USSR	251

Exercise 152 (Target time = 15 minutes)

Type the following table. Choose your own method of display.

Consumer Research Department
Customer Analysis

	A	%	B	%	C	%
Adelaide	3,334	0.68	15,626	0.65	39,722	0.53
Brisbane	6,095	1.25	18,876	0.76	55,016	0.74
Perth	4,978	1.02	17,298	0.72	48,729	0.68

Continuous matter with tables

This may include both tabular material and continuous matter (paragraphs).

1 Decide on the margins for the continuous matter.
2 Calculate the tabulated matter in relation to the writing line (which may not be the width of the paper). If you decide to use equal margins (say 2″ either side), the calculations can be done on the paper width *or* on the margins (the result will be the same).

Exercise 123 (Target time = 20 minutes)

Type on A4 letterheaded paper.

Everton Crouch

Blocked style on A4. All lines begin at left-hand margin

①
SWS/bk
①
10 March 19--
①
Miss S Carr
27 Charlotte Road
HEANOR
Derbyshire   DE7 7BL
①
Dear Miss Carr
①
HOLIDAYS COMPETITION
①

Use A4 letterhead if possible (page 167) but if not, allow 12 line spaces to the bottom of the letterhead

We are very pleased to inform you that your entry in our Holidays Competition has won the second prize - a holiday for two in Italy. All the following items are included in the price.
①

Use a left margin of 1"

You will travel by train to London and a meal will be provided on the train. One of our cars will be waiting to take you to the airport. You will then fly to Venice and be taken by car to a first-class hotel where you will spend one week. You will then be taken to spend another week at a new sea-side resort, where once again you will stay in a first-class hotel, and all arrangements will be made for your return flight and rail travel back to your home.

For the holiday we are providing you with £400 spending money in travellers' cheques. Arrangements will be made for you to collect these from your nearest branch of our bankers, and we shall inform you at a later date when you should call for them.

Fuller details of the arrangements will be sent to you shortly. In the meantime please let us know, within a week if possible, the name and address of your companion and the time of year you can take the holiday. The period must be between June and September.

We look forward to hearing from you, and we send you our warmest congratulations.
①
Yours sincerely

④

S W Simons
Manager

Envelope addressing: business letters

Varying the space between columns

In most tabular work, equal spacing is left between columns and it is essential that spacing is consistent. However, in some instances the spacing can be varied. In the example below it is important that the reader should realise at a glance that the first two and the second two columns are associated, and this point can be emphasised by leaving more space between columns 2 and 3 than you do between columns 1 and 2 or 3 and 4. This explains the leaving of 6 spaces as the centre separation and 3 spaces for each of the other two.

ENGLISH COUNTY NAMES
which may be abbreviated in postal addresses

County	Abbreviation	County	Abbreviation
Bedfordshire	Beds.	North Humberside	N. Humberside
Berkshire	Berks.	Northumberland	Northd.
Buckinghamshire	Bucks.	North Yorkshire	N. Yorks.
Cambridgeshire	Cambs.	Nottinghamshire	Notts.
County Durham	Co. Durham ⑥	Oxfordshire	Oxon.
East Sussex	E. Sussex	South Humberside ③	S. Humberside
Gloucestershire ③	Glos.	South Yorkshire	S. Yorks.
Hampshire	Hants.	Staffordshire	Staffs.
Hertfordshire	Herts.	Tyne and Wear	Tyne & Wear
Lancashire	Lancs.	West Midlands	W. Midlands
Leicestershire	Leics.	West Sussex	W. Sussex
Lincolnshire	Lincs.	West Yorkshire	W. Yorks
Middlesex	Middx.	Wiltshire	Wilts.
Northamptonshire	Northants.	Worcestershire	Worcs.

Exercise 149 (Target time = 20 minutes)

Type the above example.

Exercise 150 (Target time = 10 minutes)

Type the following table to give an effective display.

Parcel Deliveries for July

Branch	Week 1	Week 2	Week 3	Week 4
Aberdeen	1,214	1,163	1,205	1,193
Birmingham	1,357	1,310	1,338	1,287
Bradford	1,321	1,298	1,279	1,339

Type on A4 letterheaded paper and take one carbon copy.

Everton Crouch

Registered Address:
Kenilworth House
Bedford Road
Hemel Hempstead
Herts, HP2 8LJ

Telephone: 0442 17376

Our Ref M/TV/189   8 November 19--

Indented
style on
A4

Mr Sandy Jones
2 Mays Buildings
Queen Street
WATFORD
Herts, WD1 2AH

Dear Sir

                    Television Maintenance

        We are writing to remind you that the third year's con-
tract under our Maintenance Insurance Scheme expires on Tuesday,
10 December.

        You are doubtless aware that your receiver may be insured
for a fourth year's service under this Scheme, with the same
benefits to you as applied to the policy which you hold for the
third year. You will see from the enclosed leaflet that we have
now extended the Scheme to cover five years of ownership, and
this is available to all customers who insured their sets at the
time of purchase.

        We feel sure, therefore, that you will <u>not</u> allow your policy
to lapse, and we regret that contract renewals cannot be accepted
unless they are received within fourteen days of date of expiration.

        We hope that we may have the pleasure of placing your name
on our list of fourth-year subscribers and for your convenience we
enclose an authorization form and also a leaflet giving details of
the revised scale of charges.

                        Yours faithfully

                        T Chandler
                        Television Department

Encs

Exercise 147 (Target time = 8 minutes)

Type the table about EVENING CLASSES shown on the previous page.

Centred style (columns blocked under column headings — columns centred on page)

```
                     EVENING CLASSES

                 Classes held on Monday

         Subject      Time       Room

         Art          1400 hrs   62
         Typing       1800 hrs    3
         Yoga         1800 hrs   14
```

Note that columns of *numbers* may either be ranged to the left as on page 91 or ranged to the right, as here. Columns with totals should be ranged to the right.

1   The main heading and sub-heading are centred on the page.
2   To centre the columns on the page:
   a   Treat the column heading as part of the column.
   b   Decide on suitable spacing between the columns.
   c   Treat the columns and the spaces between them as one large column ('block'), ie the 3 columns headed Subject, Time and Room, plus the spaces between the 3 columns.
   d   *Arithmetic method (see page 41):*

- Count the total number of letters and spaces across the 'block'.
- Find the left margin as you have already done for horizontal centring. See pages 41-42. Set the left margin. Follow steps *d* to *h* for the blocked style.

   e   *Backspace method (see page 42):*

- Find the centre point of the paper.
- Backspace once for every 2 letters and spaces in the block to find the left margin. Set the margin.
- Follow steps *d* to *g* for the blocked style.

Main headings and sub-headings — vertical line spacing

- At least 1 clear line space should be left below the main headings and the sub-headings. This may be varied to improve the effect.
- Headings may be typed in a variety of ways eg capitals, underscored, to emphasise their importance.

Vertical centring

1   Find the number of vertical spaces on the paper being used. The line depth of both pica and elite is the same — six lines per inch.
2   Count the total number of lines and spaces required for the task.
3   Deduct it from the total number of lines available on the sheet.
4   Divide by two. Turn down this number of line spaces from the top edge of the paper plus one extra line for the line of type.

Exercise 148 (Target time = 8 minutes)

Type the example above, centring horizontally and vertically on A5 paper used landscape.

Exercise 125   (Target time = 20 minutes)

Type on A4 letterheaded paper.

Your Ref: PX202   1 December 19--
Our Ref: STL/SW

FOR THE ATTENTION OF MR. B. SAMUELS, SECRETARY

Matlock Recreation Centre,
74 Victoria Road,
MATLOCK,
Derbyshire. DE4 3DQ

Dear Sirs,

                         ACCOUNT NO. 57842

     The Inland Revenue has recently emphasised that all interest
on investments made by non-exempt clubs and associations is still
liable to income tax at the standard rate(s), as it always has
been. This means that, although a building society can still pay
or credit interest which is not subject to income tax, it must
nevertheless pay at the standard rate in addition, under its
arrangement with the Inland Revenue.

     The cost of such investments to the society is therefore
higher than that of those investors on whose interest a composite
rate of tax is always charged. Therefore, my Directors have decided,
reluctantly, to give you notice that, from 1 June next, the interest
on the account you control will be reduced by ½ per cent in order to
allow for the higher rate of tax we have to pay.

     Should the account referred to be altogether exempt from tax
because it is charitable or educational, or on any other ground, and
if you can supply confirmation of this to me, the normal rate for an
individual investment can still apply.

                              Yours faithfully,

                              S. T. Longman,
                              Managing Director.

c.c. R. James, Accounts.

Envelope addressing: business letters   76

8 Tabulation (Part 1)

Tables have a varying number of columns which are often of varying widths. In addition, the columns often have headings.

Horizontal centring

- There are three methods illustrated. Time is saved by using the blocked style, unless you are requested to use another style.
- Remember to clear all tab stops before beginning.

Blocked style

```
EVENING CLASSES

Classes held on Monday

Subject    Time       Room

Art        1400 hrs   62
Typing     1800 hrs   3
Yoga       1800 hrs   14
```

1 Set a left margin. 1″ is acceptable but it can be more. Note that in this style the table does not need to be centred on the page.
2 The main heading and sub-heading may begin at the left margin, or may be centred. Leave at least one clear line space between headings.
3 Columns:

   a Treat the column heading as part of the column.
   b Decide on suitable spacing between the columns — 3 is usually enough so that the columns are not too close, nor too far apart that the eye cannot read across the line.
   c Set a left margin for the first column (1″ is acceptable).
   d Tap the space bar once for each letter in the longest line in the first column ('subject') plus once for each space you have decided to leave between the columns. Set a tab stop for this column at this point.
   e Tap across the second column (including spaces between words, plus once for each space you have decided to leave between the columns). Set the tab stop for the third column.
   f Type the two main headings.
   g Type the first column heading and underline it. Press the tab bar/key to move to the first tab stop. Type the second heading and underline it. Press the tab bar/key again, and type the third heading at the next tab stop.
   h Type the columns: type the first line of column 1, press the tab bar/key and type the first line of column 2, press the tab bar/key and type the first line of column 3 and then press the carriage-return key. Continue in this way until the table is completed. You must type each line across the table before beginning the next.

Exercise 126 (Target time = 15 minutes)

Type this letter, which should be addressed to Mrs B J Robinson, 117 Scarsdale Road, Middlesbrough, Cleveland TS1 2WL. Use open punctuation.

Dear Madam

In ~~reply~~ answer to your postcard requesting further information regarding the use of our 'Everlast' wood and seal dye on parquet floors, we have pleasure in enclosing copies of our technical literature covering the use of these products. You mention that the floor is badly worn in parts, and it occurred to us that you may wish to have a proper renovation of the flooring undertaken.

We ourselves are contractors for floor and wood finishing and would be more than happy to advise you and estimate for the resurfacing, dyeing and sealing of your floor, without any charge or obligation on your part. If this would be of interest to you, may we suggest that you contact our Polishing Contracts Department Manager, Mr. E. W. Jackson, at our London showroom. We enclose a leaflet giving full details, together with the address of the showroom.

With regard to your inquiry about the renovation of floor tiles, we would strongly recommend the use of our cleaning solvent, which is a highly efficient cleaner for removing wax build-up and dirt from polished surfaces.

Yours faithfully,

Andrew Fyles
Marketing Manager

Exercise 143 (Target time = 10 minutes)

Type a letter to your local gas board on A5 paper, enclosing the account they have just sent you, and complain that it is asking for at least double the amount you ought to have to pay. Ask them to investigate the error and to write to you.

Postcards

Postcards used in place of letters

- Postcards may be used if the message is short and not private.
- The standard size is A6 (148 mm × 105 mm).
- Margins should be at least ½ in (12 mm).
- If the firm's address is not printed at the top of the card, it should be typed on the fourth line from the top, either on a single line or extending to 2. Either centre the address or begin at the left margin.
- It is not necessary to include an inside name and address, salutation or complimentary close.
- The recipient's address on the reverse side is typed in the normal way, as for an envelope (see pages 55-56).

Exercise 144 (Target time = 8 minutes)

Type the example below. Type your own name and address on the reverse side.

```
SMITH, JONES AND DUNN
414 ROCHESTER ROAD   SCARBOROUGH   N YORKS

Ref PM/bw                                16 August 19--

Thank you for your enquiry dated 26 July.  The matter is
being investigated and we hope to contact you within
two weeks.
```

Exercise 145 (Target time = 8 minutes)

Type a postcard to a travel agent asking for particulars of holidays in Switzerland.

Exercise 146 (Target time = 10 minutes)

Type a postcard to Mrs J Wilkinson, 29 Eastwood Crescent, Pinner, Middx, thanking her for her inquiry regarding details of bedroom furniture and saying that the new brochure will be available shortly, and will be sent to her. You are working for SMITH, JONES & DUNN (see Exercise 144).

Other uses for cards

- Cards may also be used to type index cards for filing, invitations and replies, keeping records and a variety of other purposes.
- Take care when typing on a card, as it may slip if not held in the machine tightly. A backing sheet will help to hold the card more firmly.

When typing the following exercises, remember to follow the instructions given on page 72.

Exercise 127 (Target time = 20 minutes)

Start new paragraphs where appropriate.

J. K. Smithson, Esq., 162 Mountey Road, Leicester, LE2 6PA. Dear Sir, We were informed when we telephoned your home that you would return from the Continent in two or three days, so we thought it best to write so that you should have full information as soon as you get back about a property which is just coming into the market. It is a house only thirty-five minutes from London by train, and in a beautiful area of the country. It meets most of your requirements, and although it is offered at £130,000, we have good reason to believe that it will be possible to purchase it for about £127,500, which you gave us as your upper limit in price. It is a substantial and very attractive house built of eighteenth-century brick, but completely modernized and very well kept up inside and out. There are two very large reception rooms, a library and a spacious kitchen equipped with every labour-saving device. There are four good-sized bedrooms and two bathrooms, the whole house being centrally heated and with almost new fitted carpets in every room. There is a double garage and the house stands in an acre of garden with a small orchard and extensive lawns. The property is freehold and its low price is explained by the fact that the present owners are emigrating to Australia and insist upon a cash settlement by private treaty. There is no question that it is a bargain. In accordance with your wishes we have had the house surveyed and a copy of our surveyor's report is enclosed. As you will see, the report is entirely favourable. Will you please therefore get in touch with us by telephone as soon as you return home. Yours faithfully, Alison Moyer, General Manager.

Exercise 128 (Target time = 20 minutes)

Start new paragraphs where appropriate.

Mr H. O. Nakai, 37-8 Hongo 4-Chome, Bunkyo Ku, Tokyo 113, Japan. Dear —, Your help in putting us in touch with your agents in the Far East is much appreciated. We are confident that our sales of fertilizers and other products, for the better use of the soil, have a wonderful future in this part of the world. This confidence is based upon three sound reasons. The first is that the heavy investment we have made in the latest large-scale machinery will enable us to make our products at a price substantially below that of our competitors at home and abroad. The second reason is that our supplies of raw materials are assured for many years to come since we are part-owners of the leading source of supply. Moreover, these raw materials are more cheaply obtained and more readily transported than from other sources of supply. Our third reason is that our research department is second to none. We are already two years ahead in our products, two of which are new this year and are already achieving first-class results in other parts of the world. You will see, therefore, why we look forward with so much confidence to our prospects of business in this field of export. We shall be glad to conduct business on the terms you suggest, namely a three per cent commission on the sales price of all goods sold to your agents and a one per cent commission on the same to you. We agree to pay the commissions monthly in arrear and propose that these terms remain in force for a period of one year from the date of contract or until the total sales reach £500,000, whichever period shall be the shorter. If it turns out to be shorter, then we would gladly review the terms in favour of yourselves and your agents. Yours —, Martin Haigh, Sales Manager.

Type the following letter on A5 paper, typing your own name under the signature space.

15 Mayflower Avenue
SOUTHAMPTON
SO5 4DN

14 March 19--

Garden Buildings Limited
PO Box 420
42 Lansdowne Road
GLASGOW   G6 3DN

Dear Sirs

I am very interested in your recent advertisement in
'Gardening Today', and should be glad to receive your
colour brochures on timber and aluminium greenhouses,
together with price lists.

My neighbour is needing a potting shed and has asked
me to include this in my inquiry.

I notice you mention an 'Easy Payment' scheme in your
advertisement, and shall be pleased to have all
details of this when you send the brochures.

Yours faithfully

A personal
business
letter on
A5 paper

Exercise 129 (Target time = 20 minutes)

Use A4 letterheaded paper.

MHM/LCC/Sp 75

Mrs A Shah
PO Box 18033
Funzi Road
Nairobi
KENYA

after it has been drawn up buy your solictor solicitor

Dear _____

I / appreciated the opportunity of meeting
~~was pleased to have met~~ you last Thursday.
As promised, I am putting into writing some of the points
we discussed.

+ other financial hazards ~~means~~ ✓

Every adult person ought to make a will. This ~~entails~~
appointing an executor &, in these days of changing taxation
you might not wish to appoint a relation or a friend. To
appoint the Bank is a simple matter. If you do so ~~appoint the Bank~~,
a special clause should be inserted in your will. If you
have already made a will the Bank can be appointed
by codicil. Where possible, the Bank would like to see a
draft of your will or codicil. If you are going to live
abroad permanently, we recommend that you should
consider making a new will in accordance with the
laws of your new country. , as you suggested.

upon
The Bank would be able to administer any estate which
is retained by you in this country as attorney for your
overseas executors, should the need arise. If, however, you
propose to be out of the country merely for a limited
time, the Bank will be pleased to act on your behalf under
a power of attorney.

Yours sincerely

J RICHARDSON
Manager

Envelope addressing: business letters

Exercise 140   (Target time = 8 minutes)

Type the following.

20 Alpine Gardens
CARDIFF
CF2 1YP

31 January 19--

Dear Susan

I have been thinking about holidays and am wondering if
you could possibly come away with me this year - say for
a fortnight at the end of July.

I shall finish my secretarial course at the college at
the end of June, and am anxious to have a holiday before
I start work at the beginning of August.

How about meeting me at 'Jo's Place' - the new coffee
bar in the High Street - next Wednesday, about seven
o'clock? It would be lovely to see you again and have
a chat anyway. Give me a ring tomorrow evening and let
me know.

Yours sincerely

Hazel

A personal
letter to a
friend

Exercise 141   (Target time = 10 minutes)

Type a letter to a friend from your own private address, inviting her to spend a
weekend at your home. Use today's date, a sheet of ordinary stationery and type
the envelope.

Continuation sheets for business letters

For letters requiring more than one A4 page a continuation sheet is necessary.

- When a second page or continuation sheet is required, use a plain sheet the same size and colour as the first sheet.
- Leave a margin of about six lines at the foot of the first page.
- Type at least 2 lines of a paragraph at the bottom.
- Do not divide a word at the end of a page.
- Begin typing on the fourth line from the top of the continuation page.
- At least 3 or 4 lines of text should be typed on the continuation sheet. Try to avoid the unpleasant effect of typing only two or three lines at the top of the sheet and leaving the whole of the remainder blank. The unbalanced appearance of such a page is most noticeable where A4 paper is being used.
- The setting out of the top of each continuation sheet varies with the style of layout being used, as shown below:

Blocked style

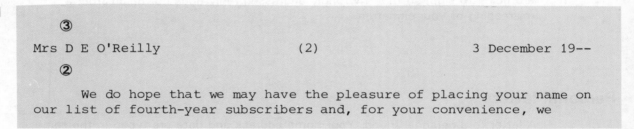

```
        ③
(2)
        ①
3 December 19--
        ①
Mrs D W O'Reilly

        ②

We do hope that we may have the pleasure of placing your name on our
list of fourth-year subscribers and, for your convenience, we
```

Indented style

```
        ③
Mrs D E O'Reilly                 (2)                    3 December 19--
        ②

        We do hope that we may have the pleasure of placing your name on
our list of fourth-year subscribers and, for your convenience, we
```

The continuation sheet begins with 1 line containing the name of the addressee, the number of the page (centred on the writing line) and the date ending at the right margin.

An alternative arrangement, given below, prevents an overcrowded effect if the name of the addressee is a lengthy one:

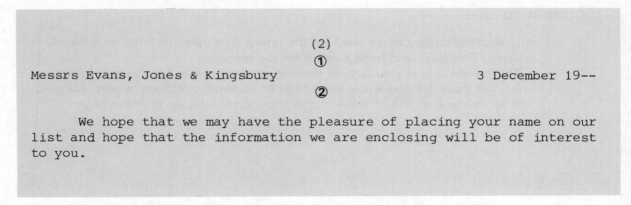

```
                                (2)
                                 ①
Messrs Evans, Jones & Kingsbury                        3 December 19--
                                 ②

        We hope that we may have the pleasure of placing your name on our
list and hope that the information we are enclosing will be of interest
to you.
```

The amount of space that is left between the continuation sheet heading details and the continuation of the body of the letter may be varied depending upon how much remains to be typed.

7   Personal correspondence; postcards

Personal business letter

This is a letter about a personal business matter to a firm. Follow the layout normally used for business letters. Your home address may be centred on the page or typed so that the longest line finishes at the right margin. Leave 1 space above the date.

The beginning of a letter to a local supplier or authority should have the official name and address and may begin 'Dear Sirs', 'Dear Sir' or 'Dear Mr Smith' — whichever is appropriate. The ending of a personal business letter is normally 'Yours faithfully' if you are writing to a company, firm or businessman, but if the addressee is known to you it may finish 'Yours sincerely'.

In an informal business letter the inside name and address may be typed at the foot of the letter, below the name/designation of the writer.

Signatures

It is a courtesy to people other than personal friends to type your name preceded, or followed, if you wish, by 'Miss', 'Mrs' or 'Ms' (below the space in which you are going to sign) so that a wrongly addressed reply does not result from a misreading of your signature.

Personal letters

A letter to a personal friend. Your home address and date are typed in the same way as in a personal business letter. Do not include the name and address of the addressee. The salutation is informal. It can be 'Dear Jack' or whatever you wish to make it.

The paper to use

Any sheet of paper can be used for the typing of a personal letter to a friend, provided it is clean and large enough for the purpose.

The A4 sheet is obviously best for long letters and the A5 sheets for shorter ones, but there are numerous other sizes of personal stationery readily available and an example of one of these is given (in actual size) on the next page.

Exercise 130

Type the examples on page 80 on A4 sheets of paper.

Practice continuation sheets

So that you can gain practice in typing continuation sheets, but not waste time typing very long letters, type Exercise 131, 132 and 133 in the following way.

1 Stop typing on the first page at the point marked 'New page'.
2 Rule a line across the page. Type the remainder of the letter as if it were a continuation sheet, or begin on a separate sheet.

Exercise 131

Type the following letter on A4 letterheaded paper. Follow the instructions above and type a continuation sheet. (Note the alternative position of the date on the first page.)

Our Ref WBG/ma   6 January 19--

Miss Olive Armitage
24 Seaview Crescent
BRIGHTON
BN1 1NN

Dear Miss Armitage

    My Committee has recently been planning the winter programme of our
Staff Sports & Social Club, and I have been asked to invite you to give us
a talk on the subject of Flower Arrangement at one of our regular weekly
meetings. These meetings are held in the Sports Hall on Wednesday
evenings and about fifty members are usually present.

    If, as we very much hope, you are able to accept this invitation, we
should like to arrange this lecture on a convenient date before Christmas.
I can, at the moment, offer you the choice of any Wednesday in November.

New Page

Miss Olive Armitage   (2)   6 January 19--

    I should mention that if you would like to illustrate your talk with
practical demonstrations or suitable films, I am sure this would greatly
add to the enjoyment of the occasion, and we can easily arrange for a
projector, screen and operator to be available.

    I am afraid we are not in the position to offer a fee for this
lecture, but we would of course pay any out-of-pocket expenses incurred.

Yours sincerely

W Giles
Secretary
Staff Sports & Social Club

Envelope addressing: business letters   81

Exercise 138 (Target time = 15 minutes)

Type the following letter on headed A4 paper in the blocked style using open punctuation; display it effectively.

W. Bainbridge, Esq.,
26 Willoughby Road,
London, W1P 3FE

Dear Sir,   26 Fairfield Avenue, Crouch End, W1P 3FE

We have received an inquiry respecting this house from a Mr. C.T. Thomas, of Muswell Hill, who wishes to know whether or not you would be prepared to let the premises unfurnished on a three years' agreement at £4000 per annum, after carrying out the following work:

(a) The house to be put into good repair, which will necessitate completely redecorating, inside and outside.

(b) The opening between the front + back rooms on the ground floor to be made the full width + height of the rooms.

(c) Electric light to be installed throughout, + electric power points to be fitted in all rooms except the bathroom.

(d) The kitchen range to be removed.

We shall be glad to have your instructions. Yrs. faithfully,

Warren Coley, Estates Manager

Exercise 139 (Target time = 20 minutes)

Type the following letter in the indented style using full punctuation; display effectively and take two carbon copies.

The General Manager
Industrial Advertisements Ltd,
425 Bourke St., Melbourne, C.1.
Australia.

Dear Sir,

We thank you for your letter of 5th December, and greatly appreciate your kind remarks regarding our system. In reply to your inquiry, we can supply you with a filing card system which has the following distinctive features:—

1. An "offset" feature which allows records to be set out of alignment for any useful purpose.

2. Metal signals available in three widths and ten colours for attaching to visible edges of cards.

3. Notes written on slips of paper can be inserted beneath the spring holder.

4. Coloured plastic signals can be used under the transparent edge-protectors of the cards.

The cards are of the four-page type, giving the writing surface of two single cards, and are easily slipped into place by means of the patented rustless steel-spring card-holder.

If you are interested we will send you full particulars of this system.

Yours faithfully,

W.A. Brown, Sales Manager.

bcc T. Woods

Exercise 132   (Target time = 30 minutes)

Retype the letter in Exercise 131 in blocked style layout.

Exercise 133   (Target time = 12 minutes)

Type the following letter on A4 headed paper. Start a continuation sheet for the second part of the letter, under the rule.

D. Johnson, Esq., 'White Gables', Lindsey Rise, Shoreham-by-Sea, West Sussex, BN4 5YB. Dear Sir, Some three months ago you consulted us about the installation of central heating for your house, but so far we have not received an order from you. You will remember that we quoted a price of £2,120, but we are pleased to inform you that we can now reduce this figure considerably as the manufacturers of the boilers and radiators we use in our work have been able to reduce manufacturing costs. You will also realize that the period June to September is not such a busy time for us, and we are therefore able to use more men for each job, thus reducing labour costs.

You may wish to consider the installation of a 'Lancashire' type boiler Model 2A instead of the larger one originally discussed. This, also, would mean a further saving. We should be pleased to arrange for our Mr. Johnson to call on you again to put revised figures before you, and we are sure that you would be interested in our quotation. We enclose a stamped addressed envelope for your reply, and look forward to hearing from you. Yours —, Barry Barnes, Sales Department.

Letters with paragraph headings

Some letters have headings for each separate part of a main subject, as an aid to speedy reference. A simple example of this kind of letter is given on page 83. Below you can find different types of paragraph headings.

Paragraph headings

Side heading

Paragraphs may be blocked, indented or hanging (see p.85). Leave 2 spaces after the longest side heading.

Shoulder heading

Paragraphs may be blocked or indented. Leave 1 clear space below the heading.

Paragraph heading (blocked)

Leave 2 spaces after the heading.

Paragraph heading (indented)

Leave 2 spaces after the heading.

Paragraph styles

Where numbered paragraphs are used to display the text of a business letter or other document, a variety of paragraph styles may be used. Blocked, indented or hanging paragraphs may be used with any style of letter layout, and the numbered paragraphs may be inset from the left and right margins for added emphasis. It is usual to leave a clear line space between numbered paragraphs (turn up 2). Four different methods of display are illustrated here. It may be necessary to set more than one tab stop, depending on the style of display used.

Example 1 — Blocked paragraphs

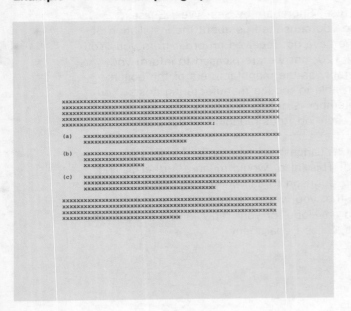

Example 2 — Indented paragraphs

Example 3 — Hanging paragraphs

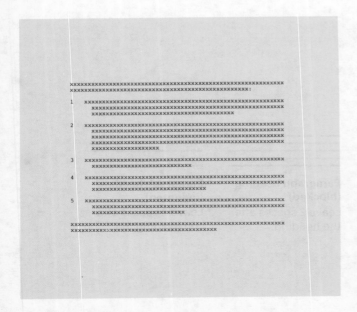

In hanging paragraphs the second and subsequent lines begin 2 spaces to the right of the first line.

Example 4 — Blocked paragraphs — indented equally from left and right margins.

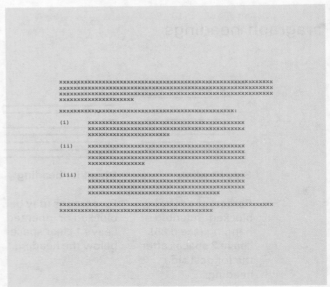

(Note alignment of numbering)
Paragraphs are blocked.

Envelope addressing: business letters

Exercise 134 (Target time = 20 minutes)

Type the following letter on headed paper. Use paragraph headings as shown.

Mr Suresh Chawla
10 Ansari Road
PO Box 7016
New Delhi 110002
INDIA

Dear Sir

CONFERENCE ACCOMMODATION

We thank you for your inquiry regarding the accommodation available at the Chandler Hall, and have much pleasure in giving you the information you require.

LARGE HALL This is a large room with comfortable seating space for approximately 1,500 people. There is a platform at one end of the hall, which will accommodate up to about twenty persons.

SMALL HALL This has seating space for approximately 800 people, with three small side-rooms which can be used as dressing-rooms or alternatively for the preparation and serving of refreshments.

LIBRARY This would be suitable for a committee meeting or a small private conference. The room is well furnished, and up to thirty persons could be seated comfortably at the conference table.

There is a great demand for the accommodation at this particular hall, and it will be advisable for you to let us know your requirements within the next few weeks. We shall then be able to offer you every assistance with this aspect of the planning of your Annual Conference.

If you require any further details, please let us know.

Yours faithfully

Miranda Johnson
Conference Organiser

Exercise 135

Retype this letter in the indented style.

Envelope addressing: business letters

83

Exercise 136 (Target time = 8 minutes)

Type the following letter in the blocked style with open punctuation; use paragraph headings. Insert today's date.

For the attention of Mr. J. Joseph, Gibson & Gibson Construction Co. Ltd., Cirencester, Glos., GL7 2HA. Dear Sirs, Hoists   Thank you for your letter of 30 December. We hope that the following information will meet your requirements: 'Moonraker' Tower Hoist The 'Moonraker' Mk. III is built for the heaviest duties on the site. Platform loads of 2.5 tonnes may be elevated at speeds of up to 50 m per minute to heights of 100 m. 'Ant Queen' Mobile Hoist   The high-speed mobile hoist with double-barrow platforms. Patented sliding headgear. Automatic safety gear. Mobile safety gates available. Please contact us again if there is any further help we can give. Yours faithfully, Service Manager.

Exercise 137 (Target time = 15 minutes)

Type the following letter in the indented style with open punctuation. Use paragraph headings. Take two carbon copies and type an envelope.

H. Johnson, Esq., Johnson & Yates, Steel Founders Ltd., Sheffield Road, Pudsey, West Yorkshire, LS28 6EB. Dear Mr. Johnson, Quality Control Courses Thank you for your letter. I am delighted to hear that it will be possible for your Area Training Officer to come to the meeting to address our staff. I would, however, like to draw your attention to the following points. Type of Student Our experience is that students attending these courses cover a fairly wide field of knowledge and ability, but the majority are likely to be junior executives who are taking up new appointments in the field of Quality Control or who are introducing Quality Control into the organizations. Title of Talk I confirm that it will be appropriate for the talk by your Area Training Officer to be entitled 'In-Service Inspection Techniques for Non-Engineering Equipment'. Date and Time The date and time for the talk are provisionally fixed for Thursday, 26th June at 1400 hrs. The course will not run unless we have sufficient delegates to justify it. I hope, therefore, that the above arrangements may be considered provisional. Yours sincerely, Training Manager.

Numbering listed items or paragraphs

Lists of items or paragraphs included within a business letter may be numbered for ease of reference. The numbers may be typed without brackets, with a bracket on each side, or with a bracket at the right-hand side only; be consistent in the use of brackets in any one document.

- A variety of methods may be used, ie, arabic numerals, roman numerals, small alphabet characters or large alphabet characters.
- Leave 2 (or 3) character spaces after the number (consistently).
- Where roman numerals are used, make sure that each paragraph heading or paragraph begins at the same point, eg:

```
(i)     The van was damaged in the accident.    (4 spaces after numeral)
(ii)    The accident has been reported.         (3 spaces after numeral)
(iii)   The damage has now been repaired.       (2 spaces after numeral)
```

- Decimal numbering is the most convenient system of numbering headings and paragraphs, particularly for long reports. Main headings or items are numbered 1, 2, 3, etc. Sub-headings or sub-paragraphs are numbered 1.1, 1.2, etc. Further sub-paragraphs are numbered 1.1.1, 1.1.2, 1.1.3, etc. Note that the full stop is essential in the decimal numbering system, even where the open punctuation style is used. (See page 122 for an example of a report with decimal numbering.)